THE CAMEROON CONDITION

Three Books on the Anatomy of Cameroon

The Mungo Bridge (First Published in 1990)

Fragments of Unity (First Published in 1992)

The Anglophone File (First Published in 1994)

THE CAMEROON CONDITION

George Ngwane

MIRACLAIRE PUBLISHING LLC

Yaounde, Cameroon.
P.O. Box 8616, Yaounde 14, Centre Region, Cameroon.
Email: info@miraclairebooks.com

Kansas City, (MO) USA
8400 East 92 Terrace, Kansas City, MO 64138, USA
Email: *info@miraclairepublishing.com*

Website: *www.miraclairepublishing.com*

ISBN-13: 978-0615621692
ISBN-10: 0615621694

PREFACE

I am pleased to provide this preface to **The Cameroon Condition** which is a collection of previously acclaimed publications by George Ngwane, that include, "The Mungo Bridge (on the West and East Cameroon divide)", "The Anglophone File (on the North West / South West Regions relations)" and "Fragments of Unity (on the problem with the South West Region of Cameroon)".

The publication of **The Cameroon Condition** is informed by popular demand as much as by the need to put the reality of the issues succinctly explored in the publications within their rightful perspective. The Question then arises, why is there a popular request for a compendium of these publications and at this point in time? Why a desire to place the issues raised in these publications in their rightful perspective? I respectfully provide the answers hereunder.

The popular demand for the publication of this volume arose from the fact that the publications in this volume, were widely read. Then and now, the publications separately or in aggregate aroused agitated public interest with varied reactions.

"The Mungo Bridge", the most popular of the publications, was a serious indictment of the tenuous relations between the Republic of Cameroon and the Southern Cameroons. With this publication, George

Ngwane became one of the very few committed writers to make a serious attempt at initiating a civil and dispassionate debate on the failed state of the union between the Republic of Cameroon and the Southern Cameroons which many saw at inception as a model for Africa unity. The writer raised not only hard questions but provided critical solutions.

George Ngwane followed through by proposing to a group of committed intellectuals in Buea the convening on the 2nd and 3rd April 1993 of an "All Anglophone Conference" to debate the future of the Southern Cameroons component territory within the union. Yes indeed, the idea was that of George Ngwane. Bate Besong, Francis Wache, Vincent Anu and my humble self-adopted it unreservedly. It is then that a decision was made to approach Professor Carlson Anyangwe, Dr Simon Munzu, Barrister Sam Elad and the Hon. Benjamin Itoe who graciously accepted to bring it to the political mainstream through the then constitutional debate that led to the ill-fated 'Tripartite talks' in Yaounde. These distinguished personalities, articulately presented the collective position of Southern Cameroons at the said talks and defended it valiantly. Unfortunately, it was ignored with the consequences that are evident in today's Cameroon.

The widely acknowledged admission of the 'Anglophone Problem' by President Paul Biya implicit in the commemoration of the 50th anniversary of the independence of Southern Cameroons and unity with the Republic of Cameroon so-called 'unification' although belated, in some ways vindicate the popular position taken by George Ngwane in "The Mongo Bridge" at a time when it was simply dangerous to do so.

The publication "The Anglophone File" based on the Anglophone regions of Cameroon to wit the North West/South West divide generated unprecedented controversy not because of its content but because that divide in itself is the very heartbeat of the politics of divide and rule that have more than anything perpetrated the subjugation of the two people. This publication was motivated by a desire to seek a solution that would take away a portend weapon of division and intrigue that kept the people permanently in a state of mistrust while both are exploited, humiliated and marginalized. The writer was misunderstood and criticized even by the victims of this form of exploitation, humiliation and marginalization for daring to raise the problem.

I travelled to Rwanda where ethnicity on the basis of Hutu/Tutsi ethnic identification is banned and criminalized and Burundi where it is allowed and encouraged. The Rwandan legislation has led to tyranny and that of Burundi has led to a robust public discourse about race/ethnic relations that has strengthened social cohesion and a wider democratic political space.

"The Anglophone File" aroused popular conscience and opened the eyes of the emergent leaders, particularly the intellectual class and the civil society to the mistakes of the past and the necessity of conceiving sustainable and enduring values that promote and protect the interest of all.

In this, the writer is vindicated by Mwalimu Julius Kambarage Nyerere in an address to delegates of the Tangayika National Union in 1964 when he said that for a better formulation of present day policies and the planning for the future, the leaders must question and evaluate the past critically and dispassionately. In so doing, the leaders must make sure the mistakes of the past are used as a rationale to detract or inhibit the charting of a better future for ourselves and posterity.

The publication "Fragments of Unity" concerns the then South West Province and now South West Region of Cameroon. Here the writer reserved the strongest criticism on his Southwest people and political class. Dr Simon Munzu, it was, who described the Southwest as a mere geographical expression. This indeed is the hard fact. It is simply unacceptable that due to the political opportunism of a few, the region is simply not only the least developed but stands the threat of losing its identity altogether. The people of the region must therefore be assertive in their demands for socio-economic and political needs and free themselves from the docility of Presidential praise singing to which they have been relegated with nothing to show for.

Ever since George Ngwane set on the journey to raise national and international awareness on the situation and condition of his people, he like most committed writers, elicited support and criticism. This is to be expected, in particular, when one writes about evolving political events.

George Ngwane has suffered serious prejudice in his career pursuits and undergone all forms of deprivations and detention for his critical publications. This is to be expected of most significant critical works in despotic regimes. On this, Wilfred Cartey writes in the African Reader: Independent Africa (Random House Inc. New York 1970 P 11) that "Any Education, any growth of awareness demands its proper sacrifice. Such is its nature: to create a contrast so startling that the past must be abandoned in favour of the future it promises or the reality it so starkly reveals". Neither George nor his people and posterity for whom he writes can escape this reality.

I therefore unreservedly recommend this publication to policy makers, academics, researchers, lawyers and the public at large to read in one volume ideas that shaped our destiny as a people and as a nation.

Chief Charles A. Taku,
Arusha Tanzania, 30 March 2012.

Contents

THE MUNGO BRIDGE

INTRODUCTION

1960 was the year that set us free from the shackles of our colonial masters – England and France. The bells of merger between two cultural heritages could be heard from Buea Mountain down to the River Benue. Our country had suffered from the greed and avarice of the colonial powers, the time had come to bury our linguistic differences under the reason of unity; the time had come to sink our cultural cleavages in the River Mungo.

It was only on 20th May 1972 that it became abundantly clear that Cameroon had become a Unitary State with two official languages English and French. The message from President Amadou Ahidjo took even his close friends by surprise. According to the former President the cumbersome federal structures of the Republic affecting the development efforts of the Cameroonian government. The maintenance of resources of three governments and four assemblies involved considerable expenditure solving which could have been used in the economic, social and cultural problems of the country.

The change from a federal to a Unitary State would according to Amadou Ahidjo permeate every facet of the National life. Such a transformation would

3

have many advantages. It would lead to a better definition and rational allocation of responsibilities.

It would simplify and clarify administrative procedures. It would lead to a more rapid dispatch of public Affairs. It would eliminate duplications, bottlenecks and overlapping within administrative channels. Finally it would result in substantial savings in consequence of the abolition of numerous administrative structures.

Any right-thinking citizen would have called this a blessing. Imagine if France and Britain were to be united. Both parties will benefit from each other and in unity they will throw their image to the lime light of international politics. We have gone through a Federal Republic to a United Republic. In 1984 the word United was dropped because from the time the "Kamerun" was applied to the territory in 1884, Cameroon has always been one nation and the division into East and West in 1916 was an arbitrary undertaking by foreign imperialist nations at a meeting in which Cameroonians were never represented and their consent was not even sought. Today Cameroon remains just "Republic of Cameroon" - a Republic that is supposed to be vibrant and dynamic, one that is supposed to give the people a sense of direction more than anything else. Yet problems are not solved by mere change of name. The Mungo Bridge therefore is more concerned with the developments and realities of the present day Cameroon - Cameroon that is at the cross-roads of two cultures. My vision of the country is one that inherently constitutes a hybrid of two cultures mixed proportionately to stand the test of African Diplomacy and brave the rough and tumble of World Politics.

It is one that has a sense of justice, a desire for peace, a sense of sacrifice and a spirit of solidarity. It is one that takes cognizance of the rights and differences of individuals where these factors are complimentary not diverse. Under such a regime, all Cameroonians must, like one people strive to work towards one destiny. For this to be achieved, we must have a renewed sense of National Integration, a renewed awareness of National Unity and a renewed concept of National Consciousness.

CHAPTER ONE

NATIONAL INTEGRATION

Paul Biya in his *Communal Liberalism* describes a Nation as a human community vitally conscious of its unity and solidarity that transcends ethnic, religious or linguistic barriers. National will be defined as the values fought for the ideals and aspirations shared by members of a nation. Therefore the word 'National' refers to what belongs to the nation.

Integration literally means the bringing or fitting together of parts to form a whole. Political integration specifically requires recognition of the uniqueness of the various parts involved in the process. It is only on the basis of this recognition that a nation can achieve its objective. Common sense therefore warns that for Cameroon to successfully integrate, the French and English speaking regions, must, as a prerequisite, take into consideration the uniqueness in terms of culture and otherwise of the two components. Genuinely therefore, fitting these two components requires decisions free from uncontrolled passion, decisions accruing from a consensus. This is the only way a whole can be regarded as a sum-total of all the parts.

For National Integration to succeed it must take cognizance of the differences inherited by the two parts from their colonial masters. The sifting process should be one of taking the good aspects of both parts and blending them. Such a country is bound to suffer from cultural and political *"metissage"* – an aspect that the Black Americans have turned to their advantage. National Integration can succeed where cohesion exists without osmotic pressure. The two parts must respect each other's differences and embrace them as a sign of love.

In our strive towards National Integration we must keep aside all the prejudices about language. Then seek for the best and let that best not be the preserve of a few but the monopoly of all.

Cameroon is united and united she will always strive to be. It is only the predicament of today that can evoke memories of nostalgia. Although the hand of history can sometimes be rewound, our country policy should not be separated by a line of two foreign languages. In fact it is at times preferable to look at ourselves as ethnic entities than official linguistic cleavages. But though we should love and feel attracted to our areas of origin and province, we should owe our alliance and love to other provinces and even more so to our great fatherland – Cameroon. How often have we let our prejudices and sentiments blind us to the realities of our nation today? Does it still matter whether oil drips from the Limbe shores instead of Douala? Does it matter whether a soap factory is built in Ebolowa instead of Bafang? What difference does it make if a complex omnisport stadium is constructed in Bamenda instead of Garoua? Our true nationalist spirits should not allow sentiments to creep into the decision making process, particularly in the location of industries and infrastructures.

For if the Limbe shores overflow with abundant oil what stops a refinery from being set up there especially if it is more expensive if not downright hopeless to connect pipelines to Douala? If all material for soap processing were littering the town of Ebolowa will it not be stupid to build a soap factory instead in the virgin town of Bafang? If all indications showed that gate-takings in football were high in Bamenda or this town was full of sports fanatics will it not be illogical to instead construct a sports temple in Garoua?

It is only logical parameters and geographical factors that can help to speed up our National Integration process. No amount of political platitude delivered on a high podium will make all men from Littoral feel secure when he knows that industries and government investments are concentrated in another part of the country just because those in the commission happened by geographical accident to come from that part.

Our love of this country should be above such bigotry. The time has come when policy makers who subjugate the rights and benefits of any Cameroonian should be considered enemies of our National Aspirations. See how much we have lost after Reunification either out of negligence, ignorance, prejudice or all of them. Every developing nation must strive to keep her transport infrastructure intact. These factors are even the shortest means to achieving our goal of National Integration for by linking all our towns together we are implicitly making our country one.

What has therefore happened to some of our transport and communication infrastructures after Reunification? Take the Kumba-Mamfe road that was earmarked Trunk 'A' Road. Is it not still submerged in mud during the rainy season and littered with dust in the dry season? Evaluating the economic viability of Kumba and Mamfe, it is disheartening to see these two towns dwindle into oblivion because of lack of adequate transport infrastructure.

While the Western, the Eastern and the Reunification roads still beg for attention, the feeder roads still remain the greatest setback in our country.

When we take into account the amount of crops wasted in the hinterland in a given year because of lack of preservation and access roads to major towns the need to re-orientate our priority is strongly felt. We may try to save our faces and images by giving the towns of Douala and Yaounde a facelift but we shall not save our stomachs and consciences by ignoring rural roads. A National Economy is a reflection of the sum total of economic values in all provinces based primarily on local products. For such an Economy to thrive, access to feeder roads must be a priority, it is through these roads that food crop produced in the rural areas are transported to the urban population in the towns. There is the Bamenda Ring Road (Bamenda-Ndop-Nkambe via Wum-Bamenda) whose reality has ended only in rhetoric. On railways so far the Trans-Cameroon railway which goes from Douala through Yaounde to the North has been a relative success. Ramifications of this network lead to Nanga Eboko, Belabo and Ngaoundere. It is sad to know that the Mbanga-Kumba rail line which links the economic capital of Douala to the commercial town of Kumba and the agricultural area of Meme Division has been virtually neglected.

River ports of Cameroon include Garoua, near the source of the River Benue, Yabassi on the River Wouri; Edea on the River Sanaga, Mbalmayo and

Abongmbang on the River Nyong and Kousseri on the River Logone. The river port in Garoua seems to be declining for natural reasons. Steamers plying up the river can do so for only two months in the year (July, September) because of the shallowness of the river at that point.

Gradually declining like the river port of Garoua but this time for some inexplicable reasons are the sea port of Bota and the creek port of Tiko in the South West Province. These two ports until recently handled the entire export trade of the then territory of West Cameroon. How much money has already been spent on dredging the estuary of the Wouri River to enable ships anchor by the side of the wharf? How can we therefore undermine a natural deep seaport in favour of one that would crumble our country's budget? When one talks of Airports in Cameroon, one often refers to Douala and Yaounde. Such great assets must be enhanced by others in the South-North line viz Ngaoundere, Garoua, and Yagoua and most recently Bamenda. These airports have always been busy only during high level administrative tours. Of the airports that are accessible to DC 4 planes, those serving Bertoua, Batouri, Yagoua are often used while Kribi and Kaele are not given enough credibility. As for the Tiko airstrip it is just a reunification symbol hurriedly cleaned when sirens are heralding the arrival of a highly placed executive. The same fate has befallen Bali, Mamfe, and Dschang airstrips accessible to DC3 planes.

The suburbs still need permanent road infrastructure and communication. A person found in an enclaved area like Eyumojock – Mamfe may enjoy watching images on television about Cameroon and the rest of the world but would certainly not have an urgent message from a relative because of Transport and communication handicap.

I fear to turn this work into a history book if I go on harping on our transport and communication problems. They only come in to show their importance in the Integration process. We must step up our roads and communication networks in the towns and villages that need them most not because certain egoistic personalities want them there.

We do not need to wait for a "son of the soil" to be a policy-maker before his soil can be littered with the fruits of development. The phrase "Son of the soil" in our tribal dictionary denotes a chap from a regional group whose main interest is to serve and be served by his trial clan. He sits in his little world called 'village' and concerns himself with no other development but that of his village. He is in fact not his country's representative but his village messenger sent to grab a share of the "National cake" to entertain his village not country men.

With our infrastructure improved on, every Cameroonian should feel comfortable wherever he is because even though "Ours is Ours, mine is mine".

The Integration process entails a careful study of the values that make up the whole. A blend of such values mixed in the right proportion will bring out our loud but hitherto meaningless cry of Harmonization.

In music the blending of discordant notes would produce poor melody. Any good musician with an intention to produce good melody must strenuously choose the different notes that would produce music worth listening or dancing to. Such is the theory of Harmonisation.

Harmonisation

Blessed by two cultures (English and French) we can choose the good elements of both mix them and come out with a real harmonized product. This is the blessing our country has but which for some selfish reasons is being turned into a curse.

At times we are left with a hybrid that has been contaminated with a bad trait while the good one has little expression. Sometimes we come out with a breed which has no bearing to the identity of the parents.

Take our legal system. Which law applies to our land? Is it the Anglo-Saxon law which states that a person is innocent until he is proved guilty or the French law that presupposes that a person is guilty unless he proves himself innocent? Is it reality possible to execute these two contradictory laws simultaneously? If not which of them has the welfare of the citizen more at heart. It is said that it is better to set ten men free when the guilty one cannot be got than to lock up ten men in search of guilty one. Up-till now our great Educationists have not come out with a lasting solution on harmonizing our Education be it at subject, syllabuses or examination level. Seminars and colloquiums have only ended up splitting the gap between the two systems since reason cannot override passion during the debates. So what do we have today?

Spill over of sentimental decisions are found in our Technical schools West of the Mungo. Technical schools that were supposed to be the corner stone of a developing nation are now falling short of recognition. Today the children in Technical schools only look like misfits or drop outs from secondary schools. What more the students come out with something between "Certificate Aptitude Professionelle" (CAP); City and Guilds and Royal Society of Arts (R.S.A.). After having attended a school that is between French and English systems they pass out with one or all of the certificates; but where do they go from there? Polytechnic – Yaounde? – No space, School of Economics – Douala? – No way. Infuriated and frustrated, they continue leeching on their parents who sooner or later get fed up. When you hear somebody talk of "The good old days" do not blame him. Think of the efficient tradesmen, builders, plumbers and electricians who occupy position in companies and ask for their alma mater. Nearly all fingers will point to Ombe. Yet today there are many of such institutions that Ombe had but few (even the present Ombe) can match the standards that the good old Ombe had.

This is partly because it had not been contaminated and nobody was forcing a system down the throats of the students. Eventually products of Technical Schools are bequeathed with no thorough educational legacy. Half-baked, half-francophonised and half-disillusioned, they come out as cheap commodity for the unemployed market. The patient and persevering ones switch to General Education where life begins again.

Another new wave is the *concour* – syndrome – A French system that permits early specialization mainly after secondary school. Such a syndrome defies and undermines the stereotyped British academic ladder that takes one from secondary school through high school to university. This helps to hasten employment even though the quality of education acquired is questionable.

Discrepancy in wages between a pass out from an *Ecole de Formation* or *Grande Ecole* (Training School) and a degree holder still calls for a lot of concern. The dilemma of Harmonisation in Education has been too long and greater attention must be drawn to this soonest.

Adoption

If we have to think that every facet of our society must be harmonized to reflect the bi-cultural nature of our country then we are just utopian. There are cases where we must fairly and freely adopt one of the two systems to tailor our general needs and interest. The adoption of such a system must be based on syllogistic reasoning, efficiency and greater output. Such a system must have been proved beyond all shades of doubt (through the setting up of commissions of inquiry) that it comes from the wish and will of the governed.

It should not just reflect the aspirations of a linguistic majority nor the dreams of a region nor worse still the dictates of an individual. To have everybody agree on a particular subject is politically impossible but if those who do not agree come from all nooks and cranny of the country then the law is morally just. But if a certain ethnic or linguistic group promulgates into law a bill that reflects their minority interest then such a law is morally unjust. A just law takes account of the wishes and aspirations of all representing the cross-section and not a simple majority. Such arbitrary decisions taken by a simple majority only widens the gulf between the East and the West.

When a system is adopted after consulting the wishes of the people, it works in the line of a democratic process of National Integration. Anything other than that is mere Assimilation – a process that obeys the law of linguistic osmotic pressure, a law that assumes that what is good for the goose must be good the gander. What we inherited from our colonial masters is not simply our political structure but regrettably some cultural idiosyncrasies. These include the conservativeness from the British and the superiority complex from the French.

These two bad habits have stalled our race towards Harmonisation. The English–speaking Cameroonian is often allergic to change especially if such a change warrants the adoption of a French-style system. He refuses that system not because it is not good but because by accepting it he has lost his own identity or should I say his British identity. Nothing is better to him than that he has grown up with. That is a typical English-speaking Cameroonian. Then the French speaking Cameroonian would not condescend to adopting the system of a numerical minority even if such a system was for the good of all.

A compromise to him is tantamount to submission, humiliation and defeat. Our Harmonization or Adoption process is not a battle between them and us. It is a search for a Cameroonian identity. The blend of good elements from both systems would provide Cameroon with uniqueness and forge for the citizens an identity that would make us proud, peaceful and prosperous.

Our haughty and unbending attitudes will never provide us with a solution to Harmonization. We are not going to bring Britain and France back to Cameroon. We are only going to use the British and French experiences to build a better Cameroon.

In such a Nation-building exercise what is paramount is the interest of our countrymen not the personal gain and frivolous honours of the leaders. It may be too harsh to believe that no aspect of our Harmonization process has succeeded in the country. Take our currency; are we not using the C.F.A franc? Arguably, the greatest success story lies in our National Football team.

That is the result of National Integration through Harmonization. For this football experience to reign all over our territory we must change our mentalities. We must regard Diang in the East as good as Bandjoun in the West.

We must respect Tchollire in the North as much as we would respect Mvomeka in the South. Geographical boundaries have much significance only to the Cameroonian map and the students of Geography.

Linguistic cleavages are only part of our History and it is our wish to turn this History into our advantage.

The most egoistic persons among us must take cognizance of the fact that nobody in this country can count on a single tribe or a language group to achieve the goals of National Integration.

Yes, the option of National Integration is a top priority; it is the *sine qua non* for the survival, vitality and progress of the Nation. For it to succeed, again, there must be a change of mentality. A genuine Cameroonian mentality based on trust, tolerance, conscience and brotherly feelings.

Bilingualism

Another catalyst of National Integration is the use of our two official languages, English and French. A linguistic phenomenon called Bilingualism.

From time immemorial, language has been regarded as unifying factor, a rallying force that brings together people with different thoughts and ideas.

How can we bring out concept of Bilingualism from the pedestal to the pedestrian? How can we turn bilingualism from a political sermon to a social reality?

Firstly, language is the property of an individual since it is the individual who possesses the ability to use the language. So no matter how much a state professes to be bilingual, the individuals of that community must by themselves be bilingual. A community is regarded bilingual when its members speak more than one language. The degree, function and alternation of the languages is however relative. It is understood that a bilingual may not be able to read, write, speak and understand both languages to the same degree.

However, it will not be necessary to acquire any language if its function is not respected. The function of bilingualism is one applied to any language viz: means of communication. No individual should acquire more than one language for the sake of prestige, honour or a stubborn sense of pride. The readiness with which a bilingual changes from one language to another depends on the situation. An individual may switch his code when he meets a person of a different language or if the topics discussed suits that language.

Since our constitution states that the two languages are official they must as well be equal in function regardless of the population that speaks either.

Relative progress has been made towards giving the two languages equal status but for certain enemies of progress who will stop at nothing to threaten the very foundation on which National Integration is built.

When our two colonial masters handed to us these two languages it looked like a blessing, for their acquisition would smoothen our social interaction and open us to the outside world where English and French seem to be the popular languages of mankind.

Again the two inherited bad habits of conservatism and superiority complex have taken our Bilingualism to the battle field. It is no more a matter of both languages in love but both languages at war.

Either because of ignorance, illiteracy, prejudice or all of them, some citizens want the osmotic law to work on our languages. How can you meet a young and energetic Cameroonian in an office who tells you he does not understand the other language? Some do not understand or speak it because theirs is a language of the majority while the others do not because their own language is trampled under the weight of domination. One linguistic group is enjoying a superiority complex; the other is suffering from a persecution complex. Yet none of them is French or an English man; none is responsible for such a historical legacy. These are the realities of history which could be turned into our advantage.

Each party is trying to play down on the other's language; where complimentarity should have remained, it is competition that prevails. Bilingualism is an advantage in the global world of discourse and diplomacy today. Let this reality sink into the ears of our directors, ministers, policy makers, and let the echoes and reverberations fall back on the errand boy, the office clerk, the hawker, the teacher, the army, the stalwart supporter, the unemployed, the student, in fact the brass and bronze of this country. Neither an Anglophone nor francophone should sell his birth right for a mess of political prestige. Let the Anglophone not deceive himself that because English language is more universal, Cameroon should become an Anglophone state or because the francophones are the majority, therefore this country must be francophonised. No. Yet when I sit among ignoramuses and intelligentsia, this strange anger of language supremacy is always vented. Guilt lurks around every mind for a crime that none ever committed.

When phrases like *"I don't understand French"* or *"Je ne connais pas votreAnglais – la"* will be removed from our repertoire, we would have gone ahead to speed up our National Integration process.

I want to look at our Bilingual situation from two perspectives; Social Bilingualism and Executive Bilingualism. On social Bilingualism, the interlocutors are interested in the message. It is more on a spoken medium and often informal. The speakers do not look at themselves as Francophones and Anglophones. They both have knowledge of their first languages and dabble in the second language even if their levels of education permit them to have phonological, lexical, grammatical and semantic interferences. Yet they alternate between the two languages without due concern for grammatical weakness. Theirs is a world of communication. Intimacy and respect for each other and each other's language impose on their sentiments and prejudice. In such a circumstance when an Anglophone finds himself in a francophone audience, he tries to join in by speaking the French language (in that situation French is the dominant language). Conversely if it is a francophone living among Anglophones he is expected to feel free with the English language. Mutual respect and the curiosity to learn the other language ties the bond between both parties. Maintaining your first language and learning the second is the guiding principle. The language barrier is not broken by snobbish sentiments or a numerical majority cult. To them language is only a vehicle of communication.

Let us turn to Executive Bilingualism. It is more written than spoken. The parties are more concerned with the code used and not what the code carries. These are mainly the "table and chair labourers" who try to frustrate our Bilingual and consequently our National Integration process. Take the military officer who insists on speaking French, types his reports only in French, does his military manoeuvres only in French, thus giving one an impression that lectures in the military school are delivered only by Voltaire, Moliere and Jean Jacques Rousseau, Take the (new breed police officer) who insists on asking for your driving documents using the French language even though his heavy English accent betrays his Anglophone origin. Take the female secretary in the public service who nonchalantly shoves aside a civil servant asking for his documents in a language that either her academic qualification did not permit her to acquire or her prejudice does not warrant her to listen to. So the civil servant goes away with his problems and ideas. Take the lecturer in the university and professional schools who denigrates another linguistic group alien to his. Take the competitive exams, recruitment, and employment that are conducted by linguistic affinity instead of academic merit. Take the politician who addresses his people in one language. Take the important communiqués and texts that are read in the radio or television in one language as if translators had outlined their usefulness in this country.

Take the journalist who has no sense of timing when it comes to a bilingual coverage. Take public notices and official documents that are written in one language even though they are meant to serve the whole nation. Take our culture screened on films and Television programmes. Watch them and you will understand what Christ meant by "To him who has more, more will be given and to him who has not, even the little that he has will be taken away". Take the state newspaper 'Cameroon Tribune' where English language is treated as a footnote. A change of mentality must come from our citizens for Bilingualism to be successful. It is the politician that can necessitate that change and only after he has gone through those changes first. The dreams and aspirations of a people are often reflected in a politician's words. To ask every politician to start learning the second language and using it effectively is mere academic injustice. To say the mastery of the two languages will be the only criterion to having a post of responsibility is a mere political blunder.

Yet there are certain key posts in this country that must be handled by bilinguals if bilingualism is a serious priority and national option. The common man's question is "How bilingual are you when you ask me to be bilingual?" How can the hopes of bilingualism be raised?

When it comes to addressing the people on important occasions, the politician must take a stand in using either a paragraph by paragraph. Bilingualism (as practised in Canada) or alternate both languages on two different occasions. By this means, no group is left out and it gives everyone a total sense of belonging.

Experience has it that those who are at ease with both languages tolerate each other as Cameroonians should. While those who know only one language look at the other speaker with suspicion and merely accommodate him out of African hospitality. If history divided us, our languages should unite us. We are first of all Cameroonians before relegating ourselves to language groups. While those practicing social bilingualism may be accused of adulterating one language, those exercising Executive bilingualism can be accused of turning our Bilingual concept into a state of diglossia. In Diglossia, there is a high language and low form. The high has more prestige and it is used more formally than the low. Other linguistics would argue that a national language be set up to eradicate these prejudices and give us an original identity. If we cannot tolerate two languages that form parts of our history then what criteria will enable us make a choice from our over two hundred ethnic groups? By then not two language groups will be at war but village may rise against village.

If we maintain our bilingual heritage within the country we shall be proud to export it to the masters that gave it to us and the entire world.

We shall then be proud to address the world in our two languages that history gave us even if it means paragraph by paragraph bilingualism or alternating between the two languages on different occasions.

Our image to the outside world must be that of a truly bilingual country not by what the constitution says but how we identify ourselves. Although a non-aligned member, our friendly ties should extend to all countries (Anglophone, Francophone) within our means and convenience. This will make more meaning to our open-door policy in international cooperation.

When I hear utterances in the radio like "Cameroon is going to host a colloquium grouping all

French-Speaking African countries" or "Cameroon will be participating in Franco-African games" I get really sick. Somebody is misrepresenting this country. We are neither a French speaking nor an English speaking country. We are a Bilingual country. When we commit such moronic blunders in our own country what do we expect of foreigner to call this country? In what area do we fit our country in a world linguistic map? I say in a Bilingual area alongside Canada, Mauritius, etc. etc.

Within the means available let us participate in Anglophone/Francophone games, summits, seminars, conferences etc. So every sports man and statesman representing this country internationally must carry with him his bilingual identity to defend the image of our fatherland. Such bilingual flexibility would place Cameroonians at the head of International Organisations.

That is what History made us, and that is what we are going to be. What we make of ourselves within the country is what others will take us to be outside. By maintaining our Bilingualism within and exporting it without, our search for National Integration will be a forgone conclusion.

If National Integration is our goal then Harmonization and a careful orientation of Bilingualism must be our means. It is only then we shall identify ourselves as members of the same family for though Anglophone and Francophone are our first names, Cameroonian must remain our family name. Our race to a strong and prosperous Cameroon lies on how psychologically prepared we are to open our hearts to and shake our hands with each other. Our blend of inherited cultures through the use of our two languages will give us the Cameroonian identity. With this identity we shall overcome the evils of tribalism, sectarianism and favouritism. We shall all hand in hand sail under the oars of National Integration across the calm River Mungo to the peaceful shores of National Unity.

CHAPTER TWO

NATIONAL UNITY

National Unity does not amount to the often restricted and passive feeling of belonging or wishing to belong to one and the same community.

It is above all a common and unanimous determination to walk together and share in a brotherly manner the same common ideals and the same hopes.

Paul Biya,
Addressing the Population of Maroua, 4th May 1983.

Unity in Diversity

Nothing best expressed this view of National Unity than such a profound philosophy postulated by the President. National Unity is a priori for Nation Building. When all the prejudices and bias are buried among a citizenry, the seeds of National Construction rise and the bonds of unity become even stronger. The abstract term of unity will remain in every political sermon as long as the people who and for whom the lecture is intended do not understand that they must put aside differences of generation, religion and ethnic origin. After all, Achebe says unity can only be as good as the purpose for which it is intended. We must understand that there is no nation without unity for it is this unity that asserts our personality and safeguards our sovereignty, even behind a complex and diverse background – such diversity that splits us into provinces. Though attached to our provinces, that spirit of love must reign in other provinces and more so our fatherland. The sense of belonging should be so high that a Bamileke feels at ease in Tombel, a Bayangi businessman prospers in Kousseri, a Bafut is comfortable in Kribi and a Hausa man gets married to a Douala girl. To take away a tribe from an African is to deprive him of his personality but such tribal solidarity should be a spring board to National Unity. Yes, in spite of such diversity a Cameroonian should consider himself, first and foremost a Cameroonian. Intrinsically this has been the foundation of any African hierarchy – Taking pride in one's village but belonging to the same tribe. There is therefore unity in diversity. This is the experience in Nigeria with states where the political, social and economic destiny of the state is dependent on the people of that state. The powers are wielded by the state Governor who in turn is responsible to the Head of State. What may be behind such a move is to avoid certain states becoming like hens laying eggs for other states to eat. Though diverse in ethnicity, such a structure still responds to the goal of unity.

It may sound jingoistic to say America borrowed this political system from Africans. Their conglomerate of states make them united as the abbreviation (U.S.A) signifies. The diverse states make them the lion of the developed nations and the elephant to the developing world. Yet such diversity has not for one reason shattered their march towards unity.

It may sound chauvinistic to say Nkrumah's dream of a United States of America stemmed from his African traditional viewpoint. Such a viewpoint that had to be contested either by people who thought such a structure (Independent States grouping to forma United States of Africa) will make Africa the Goliath of World Affairs, or by people who feared such a structure will reduce them to the Davids of match-box communities.

All in all such a unity in diversity structure bears fruits that posterity will always reap. Let us take our case where Provinces are mere geographical expressions. All fallible and infallible decision (even with the best intentions) may not be aware of the geographical, cultural and social constraints of each province.

Let us look at a certain perspective held by some highly placed citizens of this country whereby the National Budget is viewed as some manna from the Head of State, a source of personal aggrandisement and wasteful expenditure -a National Cake, no longer the National Budget, to be guzzled up ever before it comes out of the bakery. Consider when a budget is allocated to the ministry and it has to trickle down to the cornucopia of directors, through the galaxy of chiefs of services and then the array of Delegates before it may finally settle down to the people for whom the budget is intended. With such a mammoth and congested system who do you hold responsible for embezzlement or fraud?

Come to think of the fact that there are other ministries that could be attended to in like manner and one would see how much money and time one wastes because of our prevailing structure.

The National Budget may be split into provinces according to their immediate needs and development projects. Each governor scrupulously studies areas of development in the province with the provincial heads and a compromise is arrived at.

After splitting the budget into provinces they are also divided to serve the various delegations. The provincial delegate of particular field is accountable at the end of the year to their governor who in turn presents the balance sheet to the minster of that particular ministry. The budget put at the disposal of the province should generate proceeds to cater for the province and percentage brought back to the Nation Treasury.

Each province must scrupulously use her budget for the welfare of the people who are first and foremost citizens of this fatherland. This prevents the individual from looking at the budget as a government affair manipulated by who so ever because the thief is always difficult to arrest along a cumbersome line.

Any province should attain the estimated budget, must bring back two-fold at the end of a financial year and not run into deficit. The province must exploit all her natural wealth and human resources to attain this goal. So the North West with all her traditional values must sell her rich image to the world so as to sustain her people and provide some for National survival.

The indefatigable North Westerners must put their wit and energy together to produce a heavy yield for the Province and the country at large. The South West with al her enviable minerals and cash crops even with her docile and apathetic people should strive to maintain a steady proceed from her own budget.

The West Province is a show-case of ingenuity and industry – the result will be – abundant wealth in a land of plenty. No doubt some provinces are naturally deprived of minerals and other natural resources but our deep-seated African hospitality will force us to share. Through this structure, the toil and sweat of one province will not offer comfort and luxury for another province.

Through this structure, no province will lie on her glory because the policy-makers happened to have come from there. Through this structure, one Province will not be laying eggs for another to consume, yes no province will benefit from the other by confrontation but by consultation.

Through this structure our cultural values will be better expressed in the province to meet a national challenge. Through this structure the goals of balanced development and social justice shall be attained. Through this structure every province will feel the arduous task of building and that building will be a National pride. Through this structure, the spirit of competition will be high enough to provoke development but not fierce enough to tear us apart. In such a structure provinces will not be looked upon as conflicting entities but complimentary units.

In such a structure no Cameroonian should count himself an alien in another province, for though our resources may be planned by each province they are communal to the state.

At first glance one may conclude that this diversity of provinces and decentralization of power could constitute a serious handicap to our drive for nation building, No, instead they would help create the salutary concept of unity.

Our National Budget (with all its good meaning) has often fallen in the hands of people who look at government as a shadow that follows you but never meets up with you.

A strong family depends on the individuals for support. It is the sum total of everybody's effort that generate wealth and prestige in the family. So too the sum total of every citizen's efforts in the province will bring income at the service of the nation.

Major decisions (appointments, dismissal etc.), affecting the country are still taken from Yaoundé but the Governors should be empowered to take decisions that reflect the socio-economic realities of their province.

Within such a centralized structure how do you blame him for asking for a "tip" before doing a service? How do you blame him for being insolent when documents are stockpiled in front of him? Within such a structure who do you blame if you stay for one and a half years before having a salary? Who do you blame if work stagnates in the province because everyone has gone to Yaounde to chase files? Who do you blame for the rampant accidents along the Douala-Yaounde road since all roads are leading to Yaounde?

Again there are certain decisions that must be taken from the capital but they are too many that one doubts the functions of the Administrative Services in the province.

In effect to ensure success in our Public Service in this country, the bulk of the work should be shifted to the provinces. Those decisions that are pertinent to the well-being of the country must remain in the seat of power but not when every civil servant has to go to Yaounde for the lamest reason.

One of the shortcomings of concentrating power and decision-making in the capital is that a decision may appear wise on the surface but senseless in its application. Take the Magnificent FONADER building in Yaounde that is supposed to serve farmers. How many farmers can be served in such a dazzling building? How many farmers can stand the red tapes that bureaucrats make in the office? How many farmers reside in the urban cities to necessitate such an imposing tower? Great cry, little wool.

Still another flaw lies in the fact that a few may benefit when the results are good but definitely every one suffers in case of poor results. Yet another flaw in concentrating power and decisions in the capital is that development is bound to be centred only in the capital.

A visitor who casually visits Yaounde and Douala leaves with a fooled impression that this is Cameroon – all skyscrapers and dazzling. Whereas a different trip to Buea, Nkambe, Abongmbang etc. would tell him about another Cameroon - all dilapidation and sombre. Although these towns have all the potentials to grow above their ashes and embers, the opportunities and possibilities have not been given them. So a lot of focus on the capital may deliberately or unintentionally blind us to the progress of other areas in the provinces which if improved would yield positive development.

The story of rural exodus and crime wave from power concentration is too old to be said in this chapter. Such a concentration and centralization process has now turned Yaounde a city of contrast. Life in the centre of the city is meant for the bourgeois who can afford to pay cut-throat rents – those whose livelihood depends on flashy cars and cosy apartments. While those whose livelihood depend on the air they breathe are now pushed to their shacks and shanties situated in the squalors at the periphery.

Let us take a look at another area that transports our cream of the society each year to the capital – education.

In the light of our divided structure each province should be capable of managing an autonomous university that can stand any academic challenge – Each university (not university centre) should be capable of offering courses that will meet the needs of our country. A University of Buea (not Advanced School of Translation and Interpretation) in the South West would provide courses on say Journalism (Arts), Political Science, Petroleum Exploitation and other disciplines. A University of Ebolowa in the South may train students in veterinary medicine, Engineering and other related disciplines. A University of Dschang in West should in addition to Agriculture offer other disciplines that would have taken students overseas, consequently draining the country's economy in the name of foreign scholarships.

With some of the provinces having this full-fledged universities, Cameroonians will be forced to study in their country as they are exposed to a wide choice of University to apply to. As such the present brain drain is curbed, the economy is revived and unity is guaranteed. Such diversities will only enrich our academic pursuit and why not, uplift our intellectual mettle in the eyes of our admirers.

The fame in medicine from the university in the South will be matched with the fame in Journalism from the University in the South West. Both of them will be the pride of the whole nation for unity is strength. If our provincial services and provincial universities could operate like our provincial hospital (where patients are treated in their localities) then our efficiency and output will be grater. With our goal of National Integration already achieved, Cameroonians will be looking at provincial set-up like various parts of the same body. Each part has her function but still remains loyally and unflinchingly attached to the body. As the general health of the body depends on the various parts so the richness and integrity of this country will depend on the cultural, social, political, intellectual and economic viability of each province.

Things fall apart only when the centre cannot hold. Here the centre (Capital) will hold because it will be linked to other provinces by transport and communication infrastructures. These infrastructures will transform our divided provinces into a united, integrated and strong nation which believes in its unity and common destiny.

That spirit of unity in diversity shall not only make us embrace provincial peculiarities and interest but will tilt our ears to the clarion call of National Consciousness.

CHAPTER THREE

NATIONAL CONSCIOUSNESS

Franz Fanon, a distinguished Negro writer, described National Consciousness as the all-embracing crystallization of the innermost hopes of the whole people, the immediate and most obvious result of the mobilization of the people.

In clearer terms Keba Joe Yih, a reputed Cameroonian essayist says National Consciousness means loyalty to the Nation. Everything and everybody else can be sacrificed to the interest of the Nation for it is the only permanent entity. Such a loyalty does not see anything indispensable in any individual nor does it recognize any quality as the unique property of an individual. Such a loyalty has nothing to do with idol worshiping since its basic motivating force is dedication to the Nation.

A synthesis of these schools of thought leaves one with the feeling that a nationally-conscious citizen is one who cares deeply about the happiness and well-being of one's country and people. Paul Biya says "A sound development of individual and collective consciousness is indeed salutary and ought to be actively encouraged. It makes it possible for the maturity of Cameroonians to be increasingly asserted".

How can one therefore show concern and care about one's country? Definitely through the art of patriotism and responsibility.

Patriotism

If patriotism is defined as the love one has for one's country then the degree of love will be difficult to assess. Patriotism like Christianity lies in the deeds and not the sermons that individuals may preach. It is not political speeches and church attendances that necessarily qualify one as patriot or a Christian. Some assume that a good patriot is one who abides by the laws of the land whether they are just or unjust. Any breach of the law is tantamount to subversion, radicalism, reactionary, revolutionary; sabotage and other political parlance that best suit the people in power and the objective of that law.

If one were to count the number of vocal patriots in this country they will be in great numbers. These are the same persons who appear on political occasions every time, more out of fear than love for the country. They adorn their walls with portraits of the President and their shelves with books on party literature.

This is the number that envelops themselves in dresses carrying the effigy of the president. This same number attends long seminars for the love of money, applaud out of flattery and return home out of necessity. This same number says in private what they will never whisper in public.

They are around when a sensitive occasion arises, read long sycophantic harangues, recite our noble National Anthem and look forward to lavish entertainment. This lot have turned themselves into political amphibians who brave the tides of a political current and defy the winds of a political hurricane.

This lot have turned themselves into grinning courtiers who blockade even a well-intentioned leader from seeing and knowing the plight and predicament of his people. This unfortunately is the lot in whom we have entrusted the destiny of this country. True Patriotism lies in our daily activities, our commitment to take our country miles ahead of where the colonialists left it.

It lies in our ability to identity ourselves with laws that can exalt us to the altar of hope while at the same time condemning those laws that can plunge us into the abyss of despair. A good patriot should be able to distinguish between a just law and an unjust one. But how does one determine whether a law is just or unjust?

Martin Luther King says "A just law is man-made code that squares with the moral law or law of God. An unjust law is a human law that is not rooted in eternal law and natural law". In other words, any law that favours an ideological majority is just. Any law that focuses on sectarian politics is unjust. Therefore those who send motions of support for a just law must also manifest their discontent over an unjust law, for Achebe says "True patriotism is possible only when the people who rule and those under their power have a common and genuine goal of maintaining the dispensation under which the nation lives". A good patriot must replace self-interest with self-sacrifice, dishonesty with honesty, praise-singing with truth-telling and his master's voice with his own voice. These virtues must glaringly stand out not by the loudness of his voice but by the content of his character.

A true patriot will always demand the highest standards for his country and accept nothing but the best for and from his people. That is my idea of a patriot but again like any blanket term, a patriot can be defined to suit the interest of the user. Those, who siphon out the country's budget every year still pass off for patriots and would vilify those, who out of love, condemn certain laws not in harmony with the welfare of the people. The army officer who bullied you into submission for calling a "big man's name in vain" Consider his actions as very patriotic.

The politician who arbitrarily pounds on a press man for criticizing the government (should I say for threatening his position?) also argues he is doing this out of patriotism. Baseless motions of support and pious admonitions administered by seasoned politicians or their mouth pieces are entirely useless in fostering true patriotism. In fact they are only essential ingredients to consolidating power and staying close to the political kitchen.

The only gift a citizen can offer to his country is love, care and trust and what he should get in return from the country is social justice, political equality and economic prosperity. When a citizen finds his love and care paid for by injustice and depression, it provokes rejection, cynicism and despair. Take a citizen who offers his selfless and incorrupt services to the nation but on national occasions sees his boss (a moral decadent) being splashed with honorary medals.

Take a civil servant whose moral purity has been questioned by all but still enjoys appointments and promotions.

One's loyalty deteriorates when the various are uplifted and the virtuous downtrodden. One's loyalty wavers when the robber is protected and the robbed punished.

These are some of the setbacks that affect the abstract and the blanket concept of patriotism. In our nonchalant attitude towards our fatherland we have never stopped to think about our national symbols. It is more of an official routine to hoist the flag and a public nicety to sing the national anthem. Our motto "PEACE WORK FATHERLAND" in one sentence means 'For peace to reign we must work hard for our dear fatherland'. Yes, this fatherland can only be reflected on how honestly we do our work, no matter the job; from the electrician through the teacher to the policy maker. Our dedication to our work and our commitment to morally just laws should be hallmarks of our patriotism. The phrase *na government work*[1] should not exist in a patriot's language, not even the disgusting phrase *government work no dey finish*[2] can qualify one as a good patriot.

To those who face the flag during national occasions, take a look at the stripes again. GREEN - represents the rich and abundant vegetation; such abundant vegetation comes from the toil and sweat of the common man. It comes from the awareness that

---

[1]This phrase denotes an indifferent attitude of civil servants toward their job
[2]This expression indicates a lack of objective towards government work.

agriculture is the mainstay of our economy. It therefore shows that the farmer is the cornerstone of this country's development. RED - reminds us of the hard-won Independence and tickles our conscience to what strides we have made after Independence. With a unique star on it, this shows our progress from RE-unification (Federation) to a one and indivisible unit. Therefore unity must remain at all cost even if some of those who keep their eyes steadfastly on that star undermine (by their prejudices and dishonestly actions) the unity achieved. YELLOW - symbolises its wealth, its soil and the sun which provides the country with energy strength and glory. Therefore our country will be deprived of all its wealth if we plunder it or siphon it to foreign banks.

God will not refuse the sun from shining because our country is poor or her soil is unproductive. Instead, we ourselves shall refuse the sun from radiating into our hearts because the fertility of the soil had been fettered with weeds of corruption, bribery, and other social ills.

The green, red and yellow stripes are different parts but when put together they form a whole; a whole of splendour and glamour; of brilliance and beauty. Our national flag therefore reinforces our unity in diversity. The toil and sweat of each province will bring together the grace and glory of our fatherland. So as you look at the flag on national occasions ask yourself these questions:

- Have I earned my salary justly?
- Am I an incarnation of bribery and corruption?
- Have I squandered my country's wealth by acquiring what my grandchildren will enjoy?
- Do I employ because of tribe affinity and not merit?
- Have I used sectarian sentiments to victimize anybody?
- Have I sold my conscience to the devil just for personal gains and frivolous honours?

If your answers to these questions are "Yes" then bow your head in shame in front of the flag and award yourself a medal of subversion, sabotage and demagogy.

But if nay be your answer then stand tall in front of the flag and patriotically join it in the chorus of the national anthem. We have been so used to singing and listening to the national anthem that we hardly ponder over the lines. In the first verse, the first four lines pay a befitting homage to our ancestors who in their self-sacrifice built this nation for us. Their tears, blood and sweat have bequeathed us with a fatherland whose worth no tongue can tell. Then the challenge:

"How can we ever pay their due?"

We can pay her due by our total loyalty to her institutions. By our very sense of patriotism we are bound to defend the country anywhere but we must first defend our consciences before God. Unless this is done our so called love, peace, toil and truth will not bring any welfare to our children.

"Land or promise, Land of glory"

Is Cameroon really a land of promise? Yes, she is – when we look at the natural resources that abound in every nook and cranny of this country, when we look at the minerals from North to South, when we look at the intellectual material that make up this country we are proud to say ours is a land of promise.

Is she a land of glory? No. Not when all her wealth is plundered by greedy citizens, not when she is stripped bare of her natural elegance and intellectual beauty. Not when rigour and moral rectitude are no more the watch words of her children. Such a country is far from being called a land of glory. Thank God the second verse brings a glimmer of hope. It calls for unity, love and a new sense of loyalty so "That true shall remain to the last."

Every time we listen to or sing the national anthem we must reflect on the lines so we can steer this nation to the safety shores of salvation. This well required not just vocal or verbal patriotism but a kind of loyalty manifested through our actions. That is our responsibility.

Responsibility

For the smooth ruining of any organisation or community, there must be individual and collective responsibility. Individual responsibility is a link in our chain of development. When one link is missing, it affects the beauty and elegance of the chain. Those who are conferred with any responsibility can serve this nation well only by living up to it. The hawker, bricklayer, policeman, teacher, politician, all have special responsibilities whose efficiency or inefficiency will make or mar our country's progress.

The civil service is especially more concerned in speeding our development process. Those who look up to the government for a monthly income must ask themselves at the end of the month whether what they have earned is what they have honestly worked for. The civil servant should spend several hours of work and not several hours at work.

Come to think of the leisure readings that take place during working hours. Think of the incessant discussions, unnecessary phone-calls and insolent reports on how the boss has moved out *"IL a voyage"* or if he is in he tells you *"Repassez a onze heures"*. So if the boss does not take a French leave, you are welcomed by stickers on the door with the time schedule "11h-12h", "16h-18h" as working hours yet the boss is supposed to be paid 40 hours, a week.

There are civil servants as there are eye servants or lip servants. Take the announcement that a prominent policy-maker is going to visit a town. The administration suddenly remembers that pot-holes must be filled, the bushes that were invading government offices need to be cleared, caterpillars and graders once more become alive as they strenuously try to beat the deadline. A few days prior to the visit become undeclared public holidays. Shops are closed (crisis or no crisis), offices are empty for bosses are running around chasing arbitrary constructions and seeing to it that everything is in order. Then comes the D-day militants line up along the hitherto dusty road now decorated, singing songs of praise.

At the sound of sirens, a crowd is formed. Bewildered mothers suckling their innocent children, rowdy urchins, the aged and the sick all jostling to catch a glimpse of the man who has kept them waiting under the midday heat. Everything is done to make sure the big man leaves with a good impression. This is a clear case of civil servants becoming eye servants. The people can ride in dusty roads, live in abject poverty, drink stream water as long as there is no important personality visiting.

I remember with scorn something that happened when I was in Yaounde University. The former President of Cameroon, Amadou Ahidjo, was going to inaugurate the School of Post and Telecommunication Ngoa Ekele. As usual stalwart supporters were at work. All trees and shrubs were made low, dustbins that were overflowing with garbage were emptied and surprisingly the CRADAT buildings were destroyed. They were destroyed to make a better view for the President and his retinue. Here was a President who believed in the philosophy of Green Revolution and just in front of his nose were some individuals busy destroying the products of his philosophy. That is a case of somebody over doing it.

Another irresponsible act that undermines our drive to national unity is the tendency for a policy-maker to think that he should be surrounded by only his tribesman from his chauffeur, night watchman to private secretary. Security he says is best guaranteed when you are surrounded by your own tribesmen not your compatriots.

From the time you enter such a service to the time you are leaving, a national language seems to have replaced one of our official languages. When I see Cameroonians give their bodies and souls to the sound of music, I ask myself why patriotism should know no boundaries like music. Does it matter whether it is a Littoral man playing the 'makossa' you (a Bamileke man) are dancing to? Does the Bakweri woman care whether the 'mangambeu' she is wriggling her waist to is from the West Province? The sound of music has imposed on our tribal affinities. The world of reason should tower over our mother tongues. Apart from such base affinities, our search for a post of responsibility is often motivated by our insatiable appetite for wealth. No job is worth the salt unless it has a large budget for you to control or sinecures ('tips,' allowances) for you to acquire.

Even the intelligentsia thinks it is only a post of responsibility that can salvage him from his social imbroglio and economic woes. So the teacher complains every day or builds up strategies towards acquiring a post, or engages in petty trading to meet up with life. His hard-earned certificate is merely a license for securing an enviable post better than just importing knowledge to the young. This post mania has stained human relationships as power struggles and rivalry between persons have given rise to mud-slinging, blackmailing and witch hunting. Once the post is acquired they become so glued to it that they cannot dissociate it from their own personalities. Attacking their posts means attacking their personalities. Attacking their functions means threatening their positions. In the end it is not the government that is served, it is the personality. While the civil service is plagued with corruption, embezzlement, unbridled quest for wealth and all other types of unlawful behaviour intended to acquire wealth, businessmen have become famous for tax evasion, illicit trading, unlawful raising of prices, fraud, ghost projects and unholy contracts. Some businessmen may have their reasons accruing from the lack of incentives from government, poor educational orientation towards self-employment, high taxes (patent) on business ventures, reluctance to nationalize the middleman's trading sector, and the tendency to consume foreign goods at the expense of home made goods. Another section of gross irresponsibility is our disrespect for government assets. Government vehicles meant for official services are used for private trips and errands. Their maintenance depends on the budget allocated to the boss. Lifts in the ministries have become the laughing stocks of modern technology. So it is less risky though strenuous climbing the stairs today than entering a lift in our ministries. Telephones, light, water are used with the mentality that it belongs to Government and therefore does not warrant adequate care.

Yet another alarming exhibition of irresponsibility is a small group of educated elite. Those who have benefited from government scholarships to study abroad, but who in the end refuse to identify themselves with their fatherland. Having lived in a land that somebody cleaned, they prefer to remain either in out of Cameroon because they say life there is a bed of roses. When they compare our toddler's strides with the giant leaps of the western world they criticise everything we are struggling to build in our nation. Those who want our country to achieve in thirty years what America already has for three hundred years must need to think hard again. The building of the country will not rest on a foundation of idle talkers and idealists. It's a pity to discover the harm, half-baked and mis-directed western education has done to the educated elite.

It is fair and good to reach for the stars but must remember on what ladder we are climbing. Squander mania is another concept in which we excel. An average Cameroonian's dream is to go in for the best. He must ride in a sleek car, wear the most impeccable suit or dress and build a cosy mansion in order to be regarded a successful man. It is this quest for the best that has reduced our morals to the worst. My salary cannot fetch me a brand new car, yet I must have one through bribery, theft, embezzlement, prostitution and cut-throat loans. We have not yet learnt to tailor our needs according to our means. Can an average Cameroonian's salary buy him the expensive suits he wears? No stretch of the imagination would say "Yes" to these questions. We must deep our hands somewhere else to meet up.

Our birth, death, marriage ceremonies must be blown out of proportion to give our invitees the impression that medieval epicurean lifestyle has come to stay. The importance of a birth and ironically death is measured by the excess and lavish ceremony that accompanies them. The status of the short-sighted benefactor is arbitrary elevated. Our individual and collective squander mania is largely responsible for the economic mess we are going through.

We have attached so much material importance to occasions and ceremonies that people have missed the point attending them. Nobody wants to leave a seminar even one on "Economic Crisis" without merry-making. This accounts for the lavish entertainment that follows some of our endless and meaningless seminars, hasty and wasteful colloquiums, redundant and exorbitant installations, superfluous and fanfare contact tours. Workers are appointed then installed amidst pomp and pageantry. With this trend of individual and collective squander mania what does the future hold? The future will be bright when the farmer works hard, the teacher teaches honestly and the policeman has his constituent and above all the nation at heart.

The future will be bright when our consciences become our masters and judges over our responsibilities. The future will be bright when we cease looking at our country as the milking cow of the jungle but regard it like the sacred cow of the Hindus.

Ours will be a better place if the youths of today avoid the soft pillows of life and face the values they often say their parents betrayed and violated. It is contradictory to know that those in responsible positions today are now practicing the vices they condemned yesterday.

Ours will be a better place when accountability and not infallibility (the boss is always right) becomes the watchword.

Ours will be a better place when our leaders say what they mean and mean what they say, for men can truly rally behind their ladders only when they have confidence in them. This is so because it is in this confidence that men are assured that the path and actions to which their leaders are committing them are the best. The leaders must lend their ears to the wails and woes of the people. The role reversal of ears and mouths must exist between the leader and the led. Thiers must be a word of dialogue and debate.

We shall be miles ahead in progress if the men in power match their rhetoric with practical actions rather than contradictions. Slogans like "Rigour and Moralization", *Consommer Camerounais*, will mean nothing if the top brass do not set the examples. We shall be miles ahead in progress if we do not always allow ourselves to be remote controlled by our colonial powers for if colonialism was a necessary evil, neo-colonialism is the worst evil. Our society must be governed by a moral philosophy which has respect for a harmonious set of norms in the working life and behaviour of individuals and the community at large.

To quote Amadou Ahidjo *"It is the building of a society which is a community with a heart and a soul which could create the desire for responsible change and the prospect for a mastered future capable of giving destiny the tinge of a collective choice for the full development of the Cameroonian"*. This demands individual and collective responsibility. The individual struggle presupposes collective responsibility at the base and collegiate responsibility at the top.

Leadership

Divine leaders are hard to come by. Maybe one needs to combine the fiery oratory of Martin Luther King, the charming charisma of Jesse Jackson, the angelic patience of Mahatma Ghandi and the downright simplicity of Julius Nyerere.

In any small organisation people choose a leader among them to represent their views and interests. A leader therefore is not the master but the servant of the people. He must therefore not create an aura of fright or atmosphere of *laissez-faire* around him. He should not be too low to be trampled upon nor too high to be reached for.

He continuously searches for the best while his people also recognize his human weaknesses as a natural phenomenon. The fact that one is chosen among the other human beings shows that a leader is first and foremost a human being not an angel nor a devil. The only quality that distinguishes him from the others is the spirit of self-sacrifice. The people's pangs and pleasures are also his. Trapped in the comfort and confine of his cosy apartment a leader suddenly forgets the plight and predicament of his people.

To avoid every human soul from consulting and confronting a leader, every civilised government has instituted a parliament. How did the idea of a Parliament begin? The puritans felt that the rights of Englishmen, which had been gained by people of earlier times; were being destroyed in England. The English decided to choose a small group of men to speak for all the people – This group is what they called "PARLIAMENT", today parliament is the rostrum of the people. The whole plenitude of the people's rights and powers resides in it just as if the whole nation were present within the hall where it sits. In point of legal theory is the nation.

If ten million Cameroonians were to be given an opportunity to see the President, he would not have any time for other business. It is for this reason that the Parliament or National Assembly comprises representatives that speak on behalf of and for the people. The parliament is to the people as the executive is to the leader. Apart from major decisions that warrant executive veto, the parliament (legislative) speaks and the executive listens. But as far back as 1760 during King George III's reign, many leaders have refused to let representatives express their ideas in parliament.

When I look at the stride the parliament has taken in this country I say to myself a light is coming at the end of the tunnel. When I turn on my radio set and hear the speaker of parliament invite his countrymen to join in nation building by bringing back ill-gotten wealth, I know democracy is here with us.

Sometimes, caught up in his official duties, the leader may isolate himself from the people he rules. It is the parliament that bridges that gap. It reminds the leader about the people's plight. It is the country's thermometer, always gauging the temperature of the people and passing the results to the leader. It is in fact the nerve centre of the country's anatomy. When the leader takes right decisions, it applauds on behalf of the people, when he takes wrong decisions it tells him "Mr Leader, you are wrong". If these are some of the elementary functions of the parliament then one may hastily conclude that with such a structure unjust laws cannot exist in a country. Yet they do abound in Cameroon, Latin American countries, in some Western Countries and they are the Africans' daily bread.

Unjust laws exist when a leader substitutes himself for the popular will. He thinks and imagines whatever he does is for the good and welfare of his people. How can this be true when most of leaders barricade themselves away from the people they govern? How can leaders know how the people feel?

Unjust laws exist when a leader shields himself away from the people and instead surrounds himself with sycophants (mostly his tribesmen) who feed him with often wrong and flattery information. When he is surrounded by cronies who take delight in telling him what he wants to hear, the leader ends up living in a fool's paradise. A leader who turns the parliament into a functionless rubber stamp body is only dong injustice to himself for by so doing he loses a vital organ of his body – the auditory organ. He then loses contact and touch with the people and imagine what it is to move from the warmth of the masses to the coldness of the ivory tower.

When a leader loses his sense of hearing from the parliament he loses his sense of judgement over the people. He therefore becomes either a megalomaniac or an iconoclast.

Leadership by consent is better than leadership by force, for it is the only brand which can endure. Men may follow the forced leadership temporality, but they will not do so willingly. Cases all over the world show how leaders have despised the Parliament that gave them the votes and mandates. Why does a leader lose confidence in parliament? A leader loses confidence in the parliament: - when a parliament is a group of people who are not even democratically elected by the people as such they do not know how they feel, they do not know what they want. Such a parliament comprises only a bundle of physical bodies representing nothing but their own shadows. When a parliament consists of representatives who have no first-hand information about their constituency either because they do not live there of they are too busy with business contracts to understand their people, such that during debates it is not surprising to find parliamentarians from the same locality giving contradictory information about their people. Such a parliament comprises only a group of confused elements.

When a parliament is made up of people who have no national concern, it is their personal financial interest that comes first, then their tribes. Not even their provinces seem to matter much to them. Instead of speaking as a united body they are torn apart by the claws of character assassination and tribalism. In this case they are a horde of egomaniacs. When the representatives have the pleasure of applauding right decisions without having the guts to condemn wrong decisions taken by the leader, they are reduced to a swarm of servile flatterers, for a parliament should be a political incinerator burning with the heat of debates and expelling the smoke of wrong decision.

The leader of a country with all his good intentions loses confidence in such an assembly and at times dictates without consulting such a mockery of an assembly. Such a leader only respects the right of the people otherwise he can dissolve such a parliament for it is there against the wishes of the people, and when a people lose faith in the parliament, they have lost faith in the nation.

The leader of the country definitely has confidence in the people. Such confidence radiates from the fact that the words of the leader are just proposals tabled to the parliament for approval or refusal. The parliament is empowered to refuse a proposal that may endanger the welfare of the nation. The confidence and harmony between the leader of the country and assembly should not bring about complicity but must serve to enhance development. Such harmonious relationship gives clairvoyance to the leader to take stock of major successes and failures the preceding years and to earmark major projects that are of national concern and that are economically, socially and culturally beneficial. He looks at the property of the country as the property of the people. He knows leaders come and go but the nation remains. The people must never forget their leaders (heroes or villains, traitors or savours) they are all part of history painted in the "CAMEROONIAN PANTHEON." He must keep abreast of all the events of his country through his country's media (T.V, radio newspapers etc. – private and government owned) so as to know the realities than listen to the flatteries from foreign dignitaries. He must transcend the flatteries of his peers to listen to the message of his detractors knowing as Bernard Fonlon said:

> that no system on this earth is sacrosanct, noting that is the work of man lies untouchable without the bounds of criticisms, No policy can be more short-sighted, more senseless, indeed more cruel and criminal than to silence men of thought, to fill them with affright, to make them live in anguish, or languish behind bars. It is deep and far-sighted wisdom, on the part of rulers, to accept criticisms and dissent as rather in the nature of things, as genuine sings of healthy state. Indeed is should be cause for disquiet and concern to them, if nay-saying vanishes from public dialogue and debate. If they are hostile to criticisms, avid for praise, they are soon surrounded by yes-men and sycophants, cringing fanny flatterers, who deceive them, who laud their thoughtless policies, who encourage them in wrong-headed waywardness who urge them on to ruin in the end, and abandon them therein.

No other message can be clearer and more direct than this offered by Bernard Fonlon. Our leaders have that challenge. To see whether the citizens of the country are loyal to the institutions, committed to their responsibilities and whether the leaders are living up to expectations they must look at themselves in the mirror. The mirror of every society is the press.

The Press

The cardinal functions of the press are to inform, educate and entertain. Government's effort to spur journalism in the country is seen through the creation of schools of Mass Communication. Infrastructure like the newspapers (private and government owned), radio and television have been instituted to accelerate information and education.

Such infrastructure would be functionless without men and women behind them. The men and women would be mere stooges if the masses were not there to read, listen to and watch them at work. Nigeria aside, this country is blessed with a cream of reputed journalists in Africa. They are not just University drop-outs or career misfits. No, they are people of calibre and fibre. We have journalists with intellectual mettle and international recognition. There are among others, two factors that can spur or stunt a journalist's career - his very up bringing (training) and the society in which he operates. A good journalist can be made out of good training and a bad one out of an air-tight society. A good journalist looks for the truth and seeks to disseminate only the truth to people. He must be able to know and find what will make newlines and not only wait for them to happen.

Like in every trade, charlatans abound in journalism there are those that seek sensational information without thorough investigation. Such a journalist spends little or no time gathering enough information before placing it at the disposal of the masses. There are the mercenaries whose job it is, to sell their journalistic ethics for any information aimed at intoxicating, inciting and distracting the masses. There are those post-maniacs who want to earn a living by their job, failing to realise that their trade like teaching and priesthood is only a noble vocation with little financial compensation. Such maniacs are at daggers drawn to canvass for a higher post or be recognised by the authorities. There are those who fan the flames of personalities and wrong decisions; cloud the path to the truth because they do not want to part with powers that be.

These are the watch dogs who have lost all their teeth and claws because they have been schooled to listen only to their master's voice. This group of individuals have prostituted the profession and flirted with its norms that few people have faith in it. Young stars no longer aspire to be journalists because their predecessors have not realised their dreams. A good journalist feels more pleasure fighting for people who cannot fight for themselves – people who do not have the time or the know-how to be sure that their government leaders are doing what they should. He is a man responsible to his craft and to the integrity of his mind. I still emphasise that our integrity of his mind. I still emphasise that our country is blessed with talented journalists but what can turn good talent into academic dummies?

First and foremost, it is the control or permissive press. A loose press is one which takes liberties in pre-empting and precipitating government actions. That was the sad tragedy that brought death to the venerated Nigeria journalist – Dele Giwa. They are citizens of the country first and foremost and pressmen thereafter, so certain laws of the land must remain state affairs.

A loose press is when it attacks personalities than issues (though personalities provoke issues). Such emphasis must be laid on the issues not on the personalities. A loose press may instead destroy the nation it is supposed to build giving rise to anarchy. So how important is a free press?

President Lyndon B. Johnson told a group of young American journalists that when a press is free, democracy will be free. He said that no press is free, democracy will be free. He said that no professional is more important than journalism and no work more valuable than that which guards the truth. There is nothing as important to a democracy as a Free press. Only people who know all the facts are able to make good judgments. The press is the market place for ideas, and with a free press, people can make their own decisions because they can read and hear all sides of the story.

In 1760 Blackstone, an essayist wrote,

> The liberty of the press is indeed essential to the nature of a free state; but this consists in laying no previous restraints on publication, and not in freedom from censor of a criminal matter when published. Every freeman has an undoubted right to lay what sentiments he pleases before the public; to forbid this, is to destroy the freedom of the press; but if he published what is improper, mischievous, or illegal, he must take consequence of his own temerity. Thus the will of individuals is left free; the abuse only of that free will is the object of legal punishment. Neither is any restraint hereby laid upon freedom of thought or inquiry; liberty of private sentiment is still left; the disseminating or the making of public, or bad sentiment, destructive to the

ends of society is the crime which society corrects.

The press is the oxygen of the country's anatomy so it should circulate freely otherwise the country would be reduced to a state of political anaerobiosis.

The journalists and the system are tied in the same garment of destiny. It is the journalist that enlightens the masses on decisions and resolutions taken by their representatives. When an air of suspicion and mutual distrust exist between the two parties the masses stand to lose. Take a journalist who in search of truth finds a policy maker a stumbling block. Take a journalist who is being dictated on what to say even though his allegiance is more to the people than to the leaders. Take a journalist who is being promoted and favoured (bureaucratic parrots) because he gives a lot of credit to the system while his counterparts is being frustrated and despised because he does not "toe the line".

Journalism in developing countries is based on investigative reports. It is not based on subjective analysis but objective and balanced arguments. The purpose of this kind of journalism is to bring changes and to make better what is wrong. Citizens lose faith in a media that always contests issues that are confirmed by anther media. A journalist loses interest in his profession when the system can readily give information about his country to a foreign press before the local press. The journalist is embarrassed when fresh news about his country is heard abroad and he now has to spend his time defining his native land. Nothing frustrates a journalist than undue censorship or administrative control on a piece of research work painfully carried out. This provokes a rebellion among the masses who turn to foreign media in quest of what they all objective reports. There is divorce between the masses and the media when they find that their right to be informed has been prevented by a new man in the news room.

Every citizen in this country thinks he knows the ethics and codes of conduct surrounding journalism - from the police-man to the Member of Parliament. They think they know what a journalists should say so when he says what does not suit the tenets of their ideologies, they call him a subvert, a radical or a revolutionary. There is little or nothing to envy George Will, Anthony Sampson, Sennen Andriamiradi, Pierre Le Louche, Dan Rather, Peter Jennings, Walter Lippman, Dele Giwa, Ray Ekpu, Patrick Wilmot, Dan Agbese and other associated journalists of high magnitude.

We have our own like Victor Epie Ngome, Jean Claude Ottou, Eric Chinje, Alain Belibi, Charlie Ndi chia, Asonglefac Nkemleke, Patrice Etoundi Mballa,

Ntemfac Ofege, Akwanka Joe, Ebssy Ngum, Sylvester Gwellem, Charles Ndongo, George Tanni and the rest of our truth-searching journalists in Cameroon. The only difference is that the two groups operate under different systems with different definitions of a free press.

While men of the first group have brought development to their various societies because of their commitment and the openness of their society, those in the second group have tried to shape their societies but their intentions are often misconstrued by some powers that should not be. To quote ace-journalist Asonglefack Nkemleke, "unfettered journalism is the conscience of a free society. Democracy cannot survive without a free press".

Any system that stifles or stunts journalistic growth is subjected to suspicion. Such a system only perpetrates social ills and serves as an above for executive criminals. The system only exposes herself at times to undeserved attacks and give the citizens a passport to believing in unbridled rumours.

Our state of democracy and level of journalism should not permit such a state of affairs. We are a developing nation and the press is an arm of development; shutting its doors will be tantamount to retarding our own development and progress. Without taking the laws into their hands, our journalists must be faithful to public interests, sincere, impartial and decent. Such qualities can only be expressed in an open society. Such qualities can stem from a profession that does not create friction because of ethnic or linguistic background. No system should aid and abate such friction.

The prowess of a journalist lies not on his ethnic origin but his competence and loyalty to his profession. No system should reward relationship instead of talents otherwise the incompetence will give progress while the talented become frustrated and seek refuge in wine and women.

We cannot stay indifferent when our journalists are leaving through the back door or when our newspapers especially of English expression are disappearing from the market, or when our citizens are gradually losing faith in their own media. There is something wrong either with the journalists or the system. It is the masses (target audience) that can judge best.

Given the best security, confidence and assurance even a mediocre journalist can take a nation from the unfathomable depths to greater heights "such is, to quote Paul Biya, "the concern expressed by the requirement of a democratic, brotherly and responsible discussion of ideas that is open to all positive contributions, especially those which are most likely to increasingly raise our aspirations for Cameroon and to enlighten us in our united march towards progress and towards the attainment of our common goals". In spite of all odds the journalist must remain astute to his job, persevering and courageous. He must have a sense of purpose and devotion, strength of character and tolerance, a will of steel and a heart of gold. These are the only hallmarks that can take the journalist away from frustration. But if you cannot beat them, snub them knowing that even though your body will be taken to jail, your spirit will remain with the people and that's where it belongs.

Conclusion

Dear Countrymen, our way to National Unity is through National Integration. The effectiveness of National Unity would depend on a more functional provincial set-up, while National Integration's goal can be achieved through careful harmonisation or objective adoption and also giving bilingualism a fresh impetus. Then our loyalty to our country shall not only be vocal patriotism but also constructive criticisms and commitment to our responsibilities would usher in a new era. A new era with a leadership that engages the executive and the legislature, a leadership that respects our bicultural background, a leadership that is a servant to all and a leadership that listens to the conscience of an open society.

THE ANGLOPHONE FILE

or

(The Story of the gulf between the "Coastal" and

"Graffi" in Anglophone Cameroon)

CHAPTER ONE

WHERE THE COASTAL/GRAFFI DIVIDE BEGAN

Land Policy

The land policy has been a factor that has influenced the population influx of the stranger element especially of the Grass Lander (graffi) to the coastal area. It all began with the coming of the Germans to the coast between 1884 and 1961. By 1892, the Germans had proclaimed the Bakweri country (Victoria division) a German territory. There was no treaty or agreement signed between the natives and the Germans as was the case with the Dualas who signed a treaty with the Germans in 1884. Over 250.000 acres of what was then Victoria and Kumba divisions were alienated to European individuals and companies. The Germans deprived the natives of their lands and established the plantations which later became incorporated into the Commonwealth Development Cooperation – C.D.C. After acquiring land and establishing plantations, the Germans now went in search of labour. The Bakwerians who lost nearly all of their fertile land used passive resistance to challenge the colonialists. They refused to be recruited as semi-slave labourers in the plantations.

This made the Germans call them names and the most popular was "the laziest beings under the Kaiser's rule". In fact they rejected such acts of social injustice whereby their land was seized, and they were expected by the imperialists, to work on it as slaves or semi-slaves. They could not accept double exploitation. Not even their resistance under the command of Kuva Likenye could stem the tide of injustice and human exploitation propagated by the Germans.

The Imperialists therefore turned their eyes towards the Bamenda plateau where there was enormous man power and where the land was relatively less fertile. All the imperialists had to do, was, offer a bale of tobacco to the Chief and a truck load of Graffi labourers would be carted down to the coast. Each labourer was paid 47 marks upon discharge and 3 marks for subsistence. They were not allowed to take along their wives and families. In spite of the bad treatment (no palm oil or dry fish) and violation of contract (no full pay) meted out to the labourers, the people of Bamenda plateau found a haven in the fertile Coastal land. With their inherent ingenuity and industry, they worked doubly hard not only for the money but for the acquisition of land in return. They gradually sneaked in their wives from the highlands to join them in the plantations and in this way started their family expansion.

When the Germans left after the First World Ward, the British imperialist expanded the plantations and introduced people from West of the Manyu River as supervisors of their massive exploitation. The British not only sold out most of the land which the already inflated Bamenda population (by 1916 about 2265 labourers were recruited in the coast) was buying; they declared some part of the Bakweri land as belonging to the crown (King of England). With the Graffi population fully present in the Coast soil, their polygamous nature bred more children and when British schools were opened exclusively for plantation families, the Graffi children naturally took the toll. The drama of the North West population influx the South West was already set. On the threshold of Independence, the colonial masters had to "leave". The baton of land ownership virtually changed from the exploitative slave-owner to the enterprising land-labourer. Even when the Bakweri inhabitants petitioned under David M. L. Endeley (Secretary to the Bakweri land committee) and later by Chief Philip Ewusi (custodian title) for the crown lands to be returned to the natives, the Government policy of laying out native land (especially land in Great Soppo) favoured the North Westerners – that explains why the Bamettas are de facto custodians of Great Soppo area.

Meanwhile other strangers like the Bamilekes were attached to the Coast because of its fertility and the maquisard crisis. Some Bassas for example resisted being used as labourers on the own land by Germans and rather fled to the Victoria regions where they are now settling as Anglo-Bassas or Anglo-Bamis. The plantation system had retarding effects on the political mind and social structure of the Bakweris in particular and the coastal in general. Having been relegated to reserves, they lost interest in life and self-respect. Even with their education the coastal hardly climbed the rungs of administrative ladders in plantation companies, owing to the obnoxious plantation policy that only those who had started from grass could ascend to grace. After all, longevity, familiarity, experience and technical know-how were better parameters for promotions than a Ph.D. award or a son of the soil syndrome. The flagrant abuse of these parameters is testified in the management of C.D.C. and PAMOL companies. With the land and labour crisis virtually settled in favour of the enterprising Graffis, the bells of independence jingled in the horizon to usher yet another divide between Graffi and Coastals. With the advent of independence the masses of Southern Cameroons understood that a political front was necessary not only for political independence but for social justice. These desires produced two great personalities Dr. Emmanuel Mbella

Lifafe Endeley from the Coast and Dr. John Ngu Foncha from the Grasslands.

Political Front

The history of Southern Cameroon, which later became West Cameroon, hinges on the personalities of Dr. E.M.L. Endeley and Dr. J.N. Foncha. They were called to shoulder the destiny of our Anglophone history. Their perceptions and personality clashes were as distant as their gigantic and diminutive statures. Tall, intelligent and handsome, Endeley represented the pride of the Coastal person, while the soft spoken and serene Foncha epitomised the humility of the Graffi man. In 1953 both were members of the Kamerun National Congress (KNC) whose objective was to assert the identity of Southern Cameroon as a people. Alas! Two years later a split occurred between these two personalities. In 1955, John Ngu Foncha broke away from the KNC to form his own Kamerun National Democratic Party (KNDP), with the reason that Endeley had failed to maintain an attitude of "benevolent neutrality" in Nigerian Politics, having opted to throw this (Endeley) support to Chief Awolowo's Action Group (AG) to the annoyance of the KNC members. Endeley's KNC party still waxed stronger. When S.T. Muna who was Vice President of KNC also resigned from the party to join J.N. Foncha's KNDP, ethnic overtones were becoming evident. Because of this set back, Endeley was advised to rely on his people (coast). He got solace in other smaller parties found in Victoria, Kumba and Mamfe to broaden not only his political friend in his cousin Paul Monyongo Kale - leader of the Kamerun People's Party (KPP) although founded by Nerius Namaso Mbile. Through the merger of Endeley's KNC and Kale's KPP, the Cameroon People's National Congress (CPNC) was born in 1957. The following year it won elections and a ministerial government was introduced with Endeley as the first Premier of Southern Cameroons. The government was however short-lived since Southern Cameroons Independence was to be decided by Plebiscite with Endeley's CPNC option of integration with Nigeria and Foncha's KNDP option of unification with Cameroon turning out to be the only two options.

The plebiscite of 1961 exposed the inner traits of our two political giants; as campaign trails turned into artillery minefields. Endeley's option of integration with Nigeria first of all surprised the electorate for he had brought stones from Nigeria, which he claimed were shot at him, to dissuade anybody voting to join Nigeria. His new excuse of the crisis in East Cameroon made him carry his integration with Nigeria message from the slippery slopes of Mamfe were he boasted to

Mamfe people that they could never achieve the intellectual brilliance and prowess of the Bakweris epitomised of course by him, to the Grassfields where he considered the inhabitants as mere intellectual inferiors and native upstarts who could save their dirty votes since the stones and trees of Fako mountain were prepared to vote for him. As Endeley's haughty attitude gradually estranged him from the electorate, the "small-no-be-sick" Foncha blasted his unification trumpet through the Chiefs who spoke for the people, recited the Ibophobia by heart and even rode his bicycle to my sub-division of Tombel where he laid water pipes as compensation if they voted for him. They voted for him but the pipes disappeared after the results. The Tombel people have hardly forgotten or forgiven Foncha for that.

As the Plebiscite Results proved (97.741 for Endeley's option, 233.571 for Foncha's) Endeley's waxing arrogance only made victory easier for the taciturn Foncha. Even if the story that Endelites lost because they were banned from delivering any public lectures and campaigns in most areas particularly in the grassland zone, what could be said of his loss in Mamfe (33.26 votes for Foncha; 10.070 for Endeley) and his own constituency Victoria division (22.082 for Foncha; 11.916 for Endeley).

It is also alleged that because of Endeley's friction with his fellow Bakweri, Fred Mbwaye, over land resettlement scheme with the Germans, the former (Endeley) ordered the arrest and subsequent three years imprisonment of the latter (Fred Mbwaye). When Fred Mbwaye came out of jail, he joined the KNDP, got over 20.000 pounds from Kwame Nkrumah (then Ghanaian leader) to finance the campaigns of KNDP against his Bakweri "brother" Endeley. The Plebiscite results were proclaimed with Foncha victorious. Not satisfied with the results, the Endelites held a secret meeting in Bova-Buea on February 18, 1961 to force that their people (those who voted for integration) be administered from Nigeria with the simple logic that those who had chosen to eat "garri" (integration) instead of "fufu-corn" (unification) should not be forced to eat fufu corn. In another move 2000 delegates from all the fifteen clans of the Bakossi and Bassosi tribes in Kumba division assembled at their traditional meeting place Muambong on Saturday 4, March 1961 and resolved to do or die, sink or swim with their blood kith and kin the Bakweri and Balondos on the objective of partitioning the territory between those who have chosen Nigeria and those who have chosen the Cameroon Republic. The "Mwan Ngoe" called on United Nations to look at the situation considering the fact that tribal sentiments rather than a clear understanding of the issues at stake had greatly influenced the voting of Foncha option and conscious of the hazards that are inherent in the proposed vague political experiment of "unification" with the Cameroon Republic – A situation which they (Mwan Ngoe) described as fraught with discontent, rancour, bitterness and terrorism. Meanwhile Dr. Endeley and N.N. Mbile carried a protest to the U.N on the grounds that ethnic elements played a most crucial role in influencing opinions during the Plebiscite. They called on the UN to interpret the results, ethnic group by ethnic group. The ideological differences of Endeley and Foncha degenerated into personality clashes which further sowed seeds of dissent between the Coastals and the Graffi. While the Foncharians were being insulted in Victoria, the Endelites were being attacked in places like Njinikom where CPNC members were prevented from building or farming on their own land by the Revolutionary Women Society called "ANLUH" something close to "Takumbeng".

Atrocious Behavioural Patterns

The Foncha Government had not settled down to savouring its victories when the pro-CPNC newspaper "Cameroons Champion" directed by CPNC Secretary General, Motomby Woleta, took on the regime's heels. In an issue of March 11, 1961 Vol, 2 n° 14, a Guest

Writer, Mr. Z.N. Efamba, under the caption "votes do not build a nation" said inter alia.

> Where is the Foncha's talk of Cameroon Nation? Will the wild votes of the Bamenda men forge a Cameroon Nation? Lumumba tried to forge an artificial Congo Nation and failed. Let Foncha learn from other people's mistakes and will be fortified to face the future with confidence.

In the same edition of the paper, Motomby Woleta wrote "indeed, Mr. Foncha has failed the real test which is not just the empty glory of victory of the ballot box, but the practical realisation of the cherished ideals for which great men work and die".

The votes from the ballot-box had constituted a West Cameroon government but the ethnic schism and personality clashes between its architects created such animosities that the KNDP's pro-Plebiscite dream of national construction was transformed into a CPNC wish of total collapse. In fact one staunch Endelite summed it as such "if the great empires of old, Greek, Roman, Carthaginian and the more recent global empires have come and gone, surely even the midget Bamita Empire of the KNDP shall meet its sunset. Not tree grows to the sky". The KNDP government did not hide its claws for long. The most revered, Dr. E.M.L. Endeley, was arrested on two occasions. First in the house of Mr. S.T.A. Torimiro on the charge that he had caused a seditious publicity about Cameroonian money in a Lagos newspaper. Even though the case was withdrawn, the Coastals felt insulted. A second arrest of Endeley came about after being arraigned to the native court following an assault against Mr. Vincent Nchami over arrangements for vote counting. Dr. Endeley was found guilty under section 88 of West Cameroon House of Assembly Regulations 1961 and sentenced to four months imprisonment or pay a sixty pound fine in the alternative. Endeley's arrests were interpreted as a deliberate attempt to humiliate the Coastal, and the dismissal from the civil service of Mr. Eric Quan and Chief Peter Moki Efange not only marked the Achilles' heel of the KNDP regime but drove a master wedge between Coastals and the Graffi.

Mr. Eric Quan and Chief Peter Efange were among the first Cameroonians to go to Ibadan University. They were therefore the pearls on the beach of West Cameroon civil service, the pride of the Coastals. One source reports that these two were dismissed because of their contempt and spite on the KNDP government (they preferred to treat their civil matters with the Nigerian government); while another source categorically maintains that these two were dismissed following a report leaked out to Prime Minister Foncha by Chief Ngwesse Makoge that the two in question were attending Kamerun National Convention Meetings. There was a law that such civil workers should not take part in politics. Foncha used this to suspend their salaries and they later lost their jobs. Whatever reasons are advanced for their dismissal they do not change the sentimental effects they had on the Coastal/Graffi divide. From then on, according to a survey interview, a catalogue of intrigues and victimisation by the KNDP regime on the Coastals were to be registered. Mr. E.K. Martin who had been installed paramount Chief of Victoria was dethroned because he refused to carry his people to the KNDP ranks. Mr. P.E.N. Malafa was pressurised to resign from civil service to join the U.N. Information Service. The banana Trade was killed by the KNDP government because it was improving living standards of the Coastal people. The College of Arts, Science and Technology which was originally ear-marked for Kumba was taken to Bambili in 1962. The school of Nursing which was earmarked for Victoria was taken to Bamenda. The Cameroon Bank was killed through long-term loans which the KNDP representatives enjoyed. The first moderator of the Basel Mission, Reverend A. Ngolle (Coastal) gave way to a Graffi man Rev. R. C. Kangsen after which a Coastal Rev. Ediage was to take his turn; instead another Graffi man Rev. Awasom came from the "blue" to be moderator. (It must be mentioned however that such an alternative arrangements of

Coastal/Graffi leadership in the Presbyterian Church is not found in the constitution). Such serious grievances cannot be swept away as mere hallucinations for they remain the psychological scar that blurs the mind of the North West / South West Unity. The unity went sour then because while the Endelites were tactlessly hostile to the KNDP regime, the Foncharians were tactfully brutal to the Coastal people.

CHAPTER TWO

WHY THE FIRST ATTEMPT AT COASTAL/GRAFFI UNITY FAILED

The catalogue of grievances by the Coastals on the KNDP regime widened the gulf between Endeley and Foncha so much that even Ahidjo's clarion call for Unity between the two personalities first at Victoria in 1962 and then in Njinikom in 1963 yielded no dividends. Instead Walter Wilson Mbong recorded these injustices against the Coastal and formed a Victoria, Kumba, Mamfe alliance (VIKUMA) with the aim of bringing the Coastals under one thinking and surviving cap. Sedition and slander gave VIKUMA a bad name as the arch griot of the KNDP, Wilfred Nkwenti used the pages of the pro-KNDP paper "Cameroon Times" to castigate VIKUMA. In one issue he wrote "The KNDP will instead of engaging in unnecessary wastage of energy against trifles like the ideals of a VIKUMA continue to find out ways and means of strengthening the unity of Federal Republic of Cameroon".

Even Prime Minister Foncha on a visit to Mamfe labelled VIKUMA a political party designed to challenge Bamenda as a whole and warned that the KNDP would take a stand to curb the dangerous and subversive activities of VIKUMA. The father of VIKUMA, Walter Wilson was jailed in 1965 and his newspaper "The Spokesman" banned. Because of this infighting between KNDP and VIKUMA, Fred Mbwaye resigned both as Vice President of VIKUMA and member of KNDP. The KNDP's credibility was rapidly waning as Dr. Bernard Fonlon showed in his serial "under the sign of the rising sun" published in "Cameroon Times" in which he pointed out the planlessness, ideological bankruptcy and party inconsistency of the KNDP government. He was still attacked by Wilfred Nkwenti in an article "Dr. Fonlon has blundered" even though an avalanche of rejoinders rebutted Wilfred Nkwenti's narrow mindedness and short-sightedness. The West Cameroon government was in dire need of a leader who could contain the Coastal/Graffi divide that was tearing into shreds the Anglophone heritage and values. As usual, Ahidjo's government was biting and blowing, preaching reconciliation between Foncha and Endeley but practicing annexation of West Cameroon by introducing the CFA, the right side driving system, the gendarmerie, and the Federal Inspectors (J.C. Ngoh in West Cameroon the West Cameron territory). With the introduction of these French vestiges, most Coastals grew suspicious of Foncha. They thought he had sold them to Ahidjo especially as he made numerous contacts with Ahidjo without letting the Press nor the people know the content of their talks.

Towards the 1972 Evolution

Ahidjo's campaign for a one party system and a unitary constitution began as far back as 1962 but he needed the rubber stamp approval of the Anglophone leaders Endeley and Foncha. Ahidjo's design was to get the destiny of the country. Endeley and Foncha wanted one dominant party from West Cameroon for different reasons. While Foncha thought that if he succeeded in convincing Endeley into dissolving his party into KNDP, the CPNC would fade out into oblivion and his leader run out of political stream, Endeley's desire was to form an Anglophone block whose objective he could not even define. Instead he wrote a letter to Foncha saying "if we are to convince our brothers on the other side of the sincerity of our desire for a peaceful, brotherly and permanent union, we must demonstrate that we are already living peacefully and amicably as brothers here in West Cameroon. I am sincerely appealing to you to reconsider the possibility of initiating discussion for a common understanding so that we could go forward together here having resolved our domestic problems before we meet other parties in the East Cameroon".

Most Foncharians read the letter upside down and interpreted it as Endeley begging Foncha for power sharing. In fact one mighty and over-zealous KNDP leader in one of his tours described Endeley as "one who has not successfully led a party and getting him into the KNDP may mean the beginning of the downfall of KNDP". So without the contribution of Endeley, the KNDP Executive unilaterally decided in Bamenda to support the one party system proposed by Amadou Ahidjo. Nonetheless, Endeley sent a letter of congratulation to Foncha for taking such an ominous decision. I totally agree with Dr. Julius Ngoh when he says that the 1972 revolution began with the collapse of multiparty politics in West Cameroon and the introduction of one party system in 1966. Both Endeley and Foncha followed Ahidjo's one party plea without knowing that in Ahidjo's weird and warped mind one party system meant one Nation (United Cameroon), one flag (single star), one constitution (unitary) and once voice (Amadou Ahidjo's). The Endelites had given up hope in Foncha's regime and virtually courted Amadou Ahidjo as Maurice Namata (acting Editor of Cameroon Champion) once wrote "Let us see the other side of the story. The Cameroon with her unwritten constitution is a young country and cannot afford to pay for the luxuries of a Federation. A unitary system of constitution is more benefiting and adaptable to the conditions as are prevalent here. Federation is a parliamentary luxury in a democracy". Indeed our two political protagonists not only vacillated in political vision but suffered from ideological myopia. The seeds of the 1972 Evolution were being sown gradually until a man of timbre and calibre took the reins of power as Prime Minister of West Cameroon. Bobe Augustine Ngom Jua became Prime Minister in 1965 with the aim of protecting the Federation promoting the Anglophone values and healing the Coastal/Graffi wounds that were evident in the Foncha regime. In his first policy speech to the House of Assembly Prime Minister Jua said "my shield will be the promotion of the economic and social development of the people of the Federal State of West Cameroon so that through this development the general welfare of the citizens of the whole federation may be assured and secured".

Under Jua's regime, Eric Quan and Peter Efange who had been dismissed became rehabilitated. It was under Jua's regime that the major event of getting the CPNC and KNDP sign a joint statement dissolving their former squabbles and promising to work hand in glove to confront the East Cameroon UC party got on foot. Paradoxically, two pathetic events occurred, after for the first time the Coastals and the Graffi literally signed a pact of fraternity and solidarity.

The Bakossis who had so far thrown their weight behind CPNC with the hope that the party will come to power someday saw Endeley's signatory with Foncha as a betrayal. They distanced themselves from the pact and ignited the Coastal/Graffi schism. Walter Wilson who had been released from jail launched a new paper called "The Citizen" in which he raved and ranted, abused and insulted this new found Anglophone Unity. Then, another devastating political earth-quake erupted – Messrs E.T. Egbe, W.N.O Effiom, M.N Ndoke, J.M. Bokwe and Sam Mofor broke away from the KNDP to form a new party Cameroon United Congress (CUC) with the reason that the merger of CPNC and KNDP was a belated step to Anglophone Unity. Mr. Solomon Tandeng Muna became this new party's President.

Reacting to this breakaway faction of the KNDP the party's Assistant Secretary General Mr. A. H. Ekele sent a Press release that revealed that Mr. S.T. Muna, J.M. Bokwe and W.N.O. Effiom were the very ones who sabotaged early arrangements to merge KNDP with CPNC in August 1964. The release further stated "Mr. Muna knows that we all know that he is all out for power, and that he is prepared to get into it by all means. He knows that we know that he is not satisfied with being a Minister, but wishes to be something more – a Prime Minister". With the crack on the KNDP wall, no formidable Anglophone party could confront Amadou Ahidjo's UC (notice the similarity between Ahidjo's UC and Muna's CUC in abbreviation).

Ahidjo's party then swallowed the other parties on 10 May 1966, digested them on 11 June 1966 and passed them out on 1st September 1966 in the form of Cameroon National Union (CNU).

On 11 January 1968, the House of Assembly met at 5.15 p.m. and the speaker read this letter from Amadou Ahidjo "I have the honour to inform you that in conformity with terms of Article 39 of the constitution, I have appointed Mr. S.T. Muna, Prime Minister of West Cameroon..." Mr. S.T. Muna was invested the following day Friday 12 January 1968 and it is significant that the first two congratulatory speeches in the House of Assembly were made by Endeley and N.N. Mbile. To quote veteran journalist and publisher of Cameroon Review Magazine, Jerome Gwellem "The method used to remove Bobe Jua through the instigation of Mr. Muna and his CUC followers was the first signal that the Federal State of West Cameroon had gone into liquidation. Ahidjo's tactics of divide and rule culminating in the splitting of Anglophones into factions had finally succeeded. Ahidjo set the stage now to finally change the constitution to a unitary state". Apart from the internal wrangles between Coastal and Graffi that gave Ahidjo a license to kill the West Cameroon State, other external factors also contributed.

(1) Jua's steadfastness to keep the Anglophones together and his spite on Ahidjo's Federal Inspector J.C Ngoh kept Ahidjo trembling.

(2) Foncha's growing popularity with the Bamilekes was something that reminded Ahidjo of the Bamilike-centered UPC party.

(3) The Biafra secession venture in Nigeria sent a chill down Ahidjo's spine that the Anglophones unity might also lead to secession.

(4) Ahidjo was growing uncomfortable with Catholics against a background of Bishop Ndongmo's role in the Ernest Ouandie affair. He needed a Protestant collaborator (S.T. Muna) not a Catholic (Foncha) to calm his fears.

With Muna as his watchdog, Ahidjo's CNU party brought a quivering zest in the lives of Cameroonians. The party brought a new mentality (that of back stabling and slander especially against KNDP militants), a new set of values (appointments instead of election); there was confusion set among the Anglophone ranks that the Graffis thinking the Coast had been developed because of the headquarters in Bamenda while the Coastals already fed up with too much Graffi power in Buea advocated for the separation of the West Cameroon state in two regions which through the mockery of the 20 May 1972 Evolution gave rise to the Provincial expressions known as North West and South West Provinces.

Collapse of West Cameroon and Inter-Provincial Wrangles

With the one party system enforced, the unitary constitution imposed, and the two Anglophone Provinces in place, the divide and dictate policy between the two Provinces became easy. If the behavioural patterns of the Coastal (South Westerner) and Graffi (North Westerner) had distanced them to Ahidjo's favour, then the administrative division between the two provinces naturally fostered the French Assimilation policy. Clad in an aura of fear and terror, Ahidjo hired and fired Anglophones to suit his whims and caprices that any of them appointed to any position of prestige (Minister, or speaker of Assembly) was made to believe it was a privilege preserved for a select few. They were told to think Cameroonians and forget they are Anglophones; preach national integration and forget linguistic discrimination; Talk about National Unity, forget unity in diversity. They obeyed in puerile piety. They all made Allah Kuba! In front of the Alhaji that it was usual for a Bayangi to betray a Bakweri in order to become a Minister or a Metta to report on a

Banso just to court Ahidjo's Machiavellian favour. They drummed Ahidjo's fame at the expense of development in their respective regions. And so even though the North West succeeded in producing a fleet of Prime Ministers and an array of House Speakers, the Province still remains the laughing stock of national development. Even though Mamfe produced seasoned politicians and virile intellectuals from the South West, the town still occupies a distasteful prominence among the wretched landscapes in the Province. Yet the North Westerner contented himself with employing and promoting his fellow North Westerner at every opportunity that was given an Anglophone. This was not taken kindly by the South Westerner who even though with relatively more developmental infrastructures still had envied the glittering shadow of North West Leadership domination. And so while some posts meant for the Anglophones went to the North Westerner who had already entrenched himself into the system, most posts for the South Westerner went to the Mamfe man who A.D. Mengot had intellectually prepared as Director of Education in West Cameroon days. With Ahidjo dangling the carrot of appointment in Anglophone eyes each Province now embarked on a policy of auto-survival and self-protection.

The North Westerner by his conglomerating culture got the gizzard. For every post he had, he made sure he groomed fellow kith and kin to "succeed" him. The South Westerner by his individualistic nature regarded such tribal solidarity as the cankerworm of tribalism. He still believed in the clean democratic rules of meritocracy not dynasty. It is alleged that when S.T. Muna resigned from his ceremonial posts of Speaker of Assembly, a South Westerner was to take over on condition that one South West Minister was to drop his post. Apart from the preliminary scuffle between two South Westerners to hold the post, no South West Minister was prepared to resign. A North West Minister dropped his post and a North Westerner late Pa Fonka Shang became the speaker. In the eyes of the South Westerner, the North Westerner is an unapologetic tribalist and the seeds of Graffi phobia have been sown like wild oats among the post-Plebiscite South West generation by his forbears. That generation has been subdued into such a psychological complex and African political reality that the drama of yesteryears seem to be rehearsed today, even though new actors, a new setting and a new stage are supposed to orchestrate an entire new power play, between the North Westerners and South Westerners.

CHAPTER THREE

HOW THE DRAMA OF SOUTH WEST/NORTH WEST DIVIDE IS BEING REHEARSED TODAY

Multiparty Politics

If power was seen to be emanating from the Anglophone Ministers, then real policies were made by one man Ahmadou Ahidjo and those policies came from one place - Yaounde. Ahidjo quit office on 4 November 1982 and handed over to President Paul Biya. Paul Biya attempted to break away from Ahidjoism and to usher in a new hurricane of democratic rights. The floodgates of multi-party politics that were hitherto closed for twenty-four years were opened on 26 May 1990 when Ni John Fru Ndi braved the heavy artillery display, set his feet on the Ntarikon soil and read his message of freedom to the military enclave Bamenda town. Prior to the official launching of the Social Democratic Front (S.D.F), it is alleged that one of its founding fathers Albert Mukong had contracted Chief Ngolle from the South West so they could join and give the party an Anglophone twist. The Chief turned down the request. Mukong and the Yondo Black group were detained. Ni John Fru Ndi outsmarted the regime and allegations still hold that he had stretched his hand of Anglophone concern to South Westerners especially Professor Victor Mukwelle Ngoh and Dr. M.N. Luma. After initial hesitation, the former turned it down and the latter accepted. With such a shaky start could the S.D.F. have embarked to address the Anglophone problem? The party emerged initially as a Liberation Front whose objectives were to break from the monolithic character and free Cameroonians from the bondage of social injustice. Because of these goals of justice and freedom, the movement lacked an ideological orientation as a political party. It was the increasing popularity of the S.D.F due to untold and unnecessary hostilities from a jittery status quo that catapulted the movement from the glimmer of a regional status to the light of a national consensus.

Fru Ndi's unequivocal oratory had woken Cameroonians from their political slumber but the question still lurked on what programme and ideology the party had both for Anglophones who took the risk of launching the party and Cameroonians who bore the brunt of sympathising with it. South Westerners seem to have welcomed the brave change carried out but could they rely on the North Westerner again. The answer was given in the South West Province when Mr. Grieg Obenson deposited his application for registration of his party- Cameroon People's Party (CPP) with the Senior Divisional Officer for Meme on August 13, 1990.

While he was planning to launch the party in Kumba on October 13, 1990 a note reached the chairman of CPP that his party had been proscribed. Reason? He dared mention Federation in his party manifesto. This definitely reshaped the S.D.F policy of action which already was given an Anglophone tinge, a North West Mafia, a Santa brother party, a cousin affair party in descending order of parochial perception.

The "peaceful" South Westerner was advised to keep a distance away from this "trouble making" North Westerner who had first of all taken us (Anglophones) into fire and had the sole responsibility of delivering us from it. Ironically, when a thing becomes unpopular to the rest of the nation, a thing in which the North Westerner piously believes, it waxes within the province like a new moon after the rains. Labelling the party as being Graffi only sent the mbangelum beat of tribal solidarity across the four cardinal points of the province. Base stalwarts went wild in ecstatic frenzy pouring tribal instincts that go with a people suffering from an unexplained persecution. As the regime spilled ripples of threats, the party thunder only rumbled with Herculean resistance. The North Westerners enjoy this game of muscle flexing while the South Westerner stood on the side-lines, watching with unadorned awe and suspicious caution. Still, where was the Anglophone in this new arrangement? If the South

Westerner and North Westerner were to pitch tents in one party camp, how will they co-exist? This is where the federation issue came in but the S.D.F. was not prepared for that yet. Albert Mukong shared the worries of the Anglophone mind when he wrote from the distant sky of London "I believe I am a member of the Social Democratic Front. I also, think I am a foundation member of the Social Democratic Front. The party must stand out against this policy called National integration for this is what we are struggling to liberate ourselves from".

In September 1991, Albert Mukong and Siga Asanga were interviewed in New York by "Africa Report" of the African American Institute. The report published in November – December 1991 had this to say: "The SDF has yet to take an official stand on the federal structure but Siga Asanga asserts that any party wishing to maintain credibility in Cameron will have to take a position, because it is one of the most important issues in the country's constitutional history".

If the forces of North West/South West Unity were channelled within the S.D.F. during its birth, if the party took a concrete Federation stand initially, it would have arguably been superfluous to have the two or three parties from resounding echo to the multiparty blast in the South West. Even if the parties from the South West did not command a large following from their apathetic population, a look at their manifestos showed their desire to timidly face the North West/South West problem within the frame work of Cameroon politics.

Article 1 of the manifesto of the Liberal Democratic Party (LDP)[3] with headquarters in Buea and Chairman Mola Njoh Litumbe, runs thus "The Republic of Cameroon as at present constituted came into being as a result of the Foumban Concordat of 1961. Political evolution during the ensuring thirty years has led to the amendment of certain provisions of that concordat, but certain other provisions remain stagnant, apparently through a lack of political will for their enforcement. Whilst the LDP may not necessarily agree with all previous constitutional amendments effected in the past, it is considered however, that the time has come to revitalise that real spirit of the Foumban Concordat".

The Conservative Republican Party (CRP) with headquarters in Limbe and Chairman Dr. Agbor Besong took the stand that S.D.F. has always chanted that is "decentralisation of administration to enable people aspires for positions at the provincial, divisional and sub-divisional levels through elections".

As for Professor Ngoh's People's Action Party (PAP), its action ended the day the learned Professor

---

[3]The LDP and NDP parties merged on 5 September 1993 to become Liberal Democratic Alliance (LDA).

got his windfall from the Parliamentary elections. Chief Isaac Oben's Federalist ideology in the Cameroon Ideological Party (CIP) still needs to be manifested in the CPDM to which he gave his unalloyed support during the Presidential elections. The numerous parties West of the Mungo threw the people apart, each following his tribal colourings. The idea of forming a consensus Anglophone party to iron out intra North West/South West differences was lost even as Tande Dibussi wept in this piece "Beyond their legitimate national ambitions therefore, Anglophone party leaders should have West Cameroonian interests as their top priority... this is not the time to revive the senseless North West/South West feud, but the time for a historic compromise which would be possible only if we finally accept each other as we are". The truth is that party politics of 1961 and that of 1990 were different. It was not only necessary to gun for Etoudi palace since there was no power in "the Schloss" in Buea, it was vital to be in control of one's own development in one's own province as well. So while the S.D.F. attracted most Cameroonians including South Westerners, most North Westerners hardly identified themselves with parties based in the South West. Even before its party re-organisation in the South West in March 1993, fears were that those in charge did not represent the natives and would be indifferent to the native interest. The re-organisation of the Provincial branch has relatively allayed those fears. The South Westerners, conscious of this danger embarked sometime on a dominant party formation that will check blatant abuse by non-natives. It is still to be realised. Detractors and slanders took advantage of this party rift to spend every ounce of their energy and every iota of their intelligence to keep the North West and South West at bay. Memoranda and letters infiltrated in the Southwest, some carrying the purported signature of Ni Fru Ndi who is alleged to have written a letter to Dr. Tchwenko on how the North Westerner planned to exploit the South Westerner in the case of election victory. Another one purported to have been written by Metta Elements directed hostilities against the South Westerner reminiscent of the KNDP days. The stage directors calculated every diabolic move to put the North West/South West at daggers drawn. Their fire-fighting was not fuelled by the ordinary North Westerner or South Westerner. The people of the North West and South West were mere victims of the bizarre machinations of power play existing between the ruling and the opposition cliques, in the new multiparty set up.

Pressure Groups

South West Elites Association (SWELA) was born with among one of its six noble objectives as found in section 3 of its constitution paragraph (a) to promote the socio-economic development of the South West Province in line with Government act". To some, SWELA had come to give them administrative promotion and political prominence; to others; VIKUMA had been reassured and the time for "Graffi" domination was over. Some elites in the Association sparked an unprecedented display of fratricidal atrocity and an unmitigated assault on the people's sensibilities. While some masses joined the hysteria, others could not understand the real vision of SWELA. Late A.T. Enaw's vision of "turning SWELA into an economic factor for the development of the South West" became hazy. The first test was the Limbe urban Council main market contract given to Mr. Bongam Isa, then the Muyuka Poultry Centre, then PAMOL. In each case passion and rage have prevailed where diplomacy and level headedness would have done the trick. While the gong of solidarity was rung, party militants garbed in SWELAN suits struck the note of vendetta. SWELA is an association for the development of the South West; in this pursuit lots of factors must be taken into consideration including the input of stranger elements who have come to stay as is natural with Coastal towns.

The influx and cosmopolitan nature of Coastal towns is a historical reality and how the stranger elements are checked would paradoxically determine the development of the town. Leaving development issues to frantically pursue domination issues has been the bane of SWELA's policy. Its advocacy for a ten-state Federation is in line with its provincial protection just like CAM's advocacy for a two-stated Federation as found in Article 5 of its constitution "to restore the statehood of Southern Cameroons with autonomous provinces" is in line with its Sovereign protection. Detractors again have capitalised on the magic numbers of ten and two to keep the South Westerner and North Westerner apart. Even though CAM's two successive Chairmen Chief Enonchong and Ambassador Martin Epie have been from the South West, the psychological and persecution complex is far from being over. While the North Westerner needs a politico-therapeutic treatment to live with the South Westerner, the South Westerner needs a psychotherapy treatment to know how to adjust with the North Westerner.

While some South Westerners are carrying out anti-campaigns against the North Westerners, the latter are giving room for confirming these fears. It is reported that after Presidential elections in 1992 some excited S.D.F stalwarts in Tombel went haywire promising hell to the neighbourhood if their party won elections. The lack of democratic education and the lack of the virtue of tolerance have relegated the North West/South West relationship into the abyss of intimidation and brutality. This will not help bridge the widening gulf. SWELA painted a sectionalist picture of itself, CAM's composition of mostly S.D.F. militants sent a wrong signal to the public, there was a need for a pressure group to emerge- a pressure group that was a rainbow coalition, embracing all yearnings yet larger than partisan sentiments. When the Anglophone Conference (AAC) therefore burst into prominence on 2 and 3 April 1993, it was like a Moses in Egypt. A.A.C.'s role was to give Anglophones their legitimate right irrespective of their mutual differences. That these differences exist is no gain saying. Nobody should be oblivious or indifferent to them. But it takes the will of a people to subdue their differences temporally in search of common goal. It will be fool hardly to believe that one can change one's behaviour overnight but good laws can regulate bad behaviour. The convenors of A.A.C. (Elad, Munzu and Anyangwe) therefore had the vision of Bobe Ngom Jua which was that of the North West and South West facing the constitutional conference as a united people. CAM will always exist even when a two or ten state federation is inscribed in the constitution in order to serve as watchdogs of Anglophone interest.

SWELA will always exist even when two or ten state Federation is inscribed in the constitution in order to serve as watchdogs of South West interests. But

A.A.C.[4] has a noble role today to reiterate in a constitutional manner, the statehood of the Anglophones and the rights of minority groups from North to East, West to South. Detractors and pseudo-intellectuals have deliberately failed to realise this differences and malicious tags are being peddled to hang the A.A.C. No army, no matter how strong can conquer its own people. Detractors, in the name of opinion leaders and elites are at work espousing the destructive maxim of "divided, we stand". A ludicrous "njangi" group called NOWELA first erected the tower of Babel when they convened a meeting with a purpose they could not even define. It was no doubt therefore that the meeting was turned into a Sunday Muea market scene. The torpedo of this NOWELA Conference like the tragedy of the Kumba SWELA conference set a new wind blowing, and a new message blasting - a new wind of solidarity and a new message of hope. For out of every North West/South West divide must be born a visionary whose task is to bridge the gap that would take the Anglophone people from the mountain top of Mount Mary to the Promised Land of Federalism. Behind every frustrating experience lies a glimmer of solace that only as a people can the plight of a people be addressed. KNDP was seen as a hostile Graffi party;

---

[4]On 28th may 1994, the A.A.C. assumed a new name "the Anglophone National Council (ANC)". Then on August 6th 1994 it got another name Southern Cameroon Peoples Council (SCPC).

S.D.F is seen as an over-bearing North West party; VIKUMA was seen as a Coastal off shoot of the CPNC; **SWELA**[5] is seen as an appendage of the CPDM; CAM is seen as a surrogate of the S.D.F; and even A.A.C. today is being smeared by parochial prattlers.

The North West/South West history is an intricate web of sterile global suspicion. The task ahead therefore is not only for all of us to go through a period of self-examination and introspection, but more so a time when opinion leaders and the Press have a valuable role to play so that with the gulf between the North West and South West we must frankly and fairly build bridges instead of walls.

---

[5]Two factions of SWELA have now emerged. One created on 18 December 1993 in Lebialem and led by Martin Nkemngu; the other created on 25 March 1994 in Kumba led by Nnoko Mbelle

CHAPTER FOUR

WHY WE MUST BUILD BRIDGES INSTEAD OF WALLS

There is therefore a Northwest/Southwest divide. This is what constitutes the Anglophone file. Anybody ignoring this will not only be subverting Anglophone Unity but will be as hypocritical as a Francophone who ignores an Anglophone/Francophone divide. The Northwest/Southwest divide is built in the psychology of the people; it is one that has left scars in the minds of the old. It is indeed the bitter memories of a fratricidal conflict, provoked by personality clashes, escalated by diverse behavioural patterns and exploited by bread and butter politicians. It is a case of a breach of trust and crisis of confidence between two brothers who are nonetheless bound to share a common vision if they must avoid an imminent cultural holocaust. After charting a course full of bends is not our duty to make the paths straight? The weary winner of yesteryears must produce a common stand of sublime spring. A look back into our history shows that we (North West/South West) all blundered. Some blundered more; others blundered less. But we all blundered. Some blundered by actively making things go wrong (others blundered by passively seeing things go wrong). It is our collective duty therefore to make things go right now.

Self-Examination

Etekele Endeley once made this remark "like it or not, the North Westerner will always be 'hot blooded', wary of making concessions when he thinks he is right; a born fighter and an uncompromising radical while the South Westerner will always be a 'Gentleman' ready for conciliation and concessions, even when he knows the other party is wrong. In short he is a dedicated moderate". We all want National Unity but we need union with ourselves first and then with the rest of the nation. To this effect the North Westerner must be seen to have trimmed his excesses and abuses. He must be seen to have respect for the Southwest territory if the creed of Provincial Autonomy is to be realised. He must be seen to accommodate his South West brother given the unparalleled liberal hospitality of the latter. He must be seen to have the democratic virtue of tolerance and fair play in his political and social agenda. He must be seen to make a clear difference between Provincial Solidarity and tribal discrimination. He must be seen to have moved from the desert of caustic invectives and vile machinations to the oasis of openness and honesty. The North West opinion leader and elite have the supreme duty of educating and if need be reprimanding its masses when the cup of irrational hysteria spills over. For the opinion leaders and elite to ignore and even defend the wanton and erratic behavioural pattern of their kith and kin will not only lead to an interpretation of complacency but also that of complicity. Where are the Anglo-Saxon values that we all talk about? Our new unity should be based on the principle of "ours is ours", but mine is mine. We are quite aware that to change one's mentality and behaviour is an uphill task and so laws within a constitution are supposed to act as safeguards and safety valves in the conduct of human affairs but like the Chinese Saga Confucius once said "Lead the people by laws and regulate them by penalties, and the people will try to keep out of jail, but will have no sense of shame. Lead the people by virtue and restrain them by the rules of decorum, and the people will have a sense of shame, and moreover will become good". On the dawn of a new dispensation, the South Westerner like the North Westerner must brace himself for the challenges that lie ahead. No people, no matter how traumatised and marginalised should remain stuck in the mire of hallucinations.

African Americans after their slavery and Africans after colonialism are still forging ahead. The Southwesterner must break free from his psychological shackles and persecution complex and face with optimism not cynicism the fierce competition that lurks in the horizon. He must face the blatant truth that he may never avoid the stranger element and it is not by puerile jitters, escapist theories and futile shadow boxing that he will make his voice heard, his identity asserted, his personality felt and his rights protected. It is not only by bequeathing to the younger generation the horrors of the past that the South West will assume its deserved role of leadership in the future. The South Westerner must look into himself and stand up. Is the South West not in itself a fragment of internal strife? It is alleged that when the school of sports was earmarked for Buea, Kumba raised hell and because of the wrangling, the school of sports went to Bamenda. That has been true with ports as well. At the dawn of multiparty politics, the South Westerner dispersed his energies into other parties forgetting that he had to consolidate his own constituency with a dominant party that would protect his interest. Even the parties based in the South West Province have poor following largely because of the apathetic, docile and indifferent people. A people that are politically sedative cannot be economically active. A house divided in itself cannot weather external storm.

Is the South West not in itself a purveyor for self-destruction? A province that glories in personal egos and individualism? Others groom their kith and kin; the South Westerner acts as if he should be the unique baobab in the forest. When blames are heaped on the mal-practices of the KNDP government were South Westerners not part of that government? Is it not true that the KNDP crisis that led to the formation of CUC party and liquidation of West Cameroon was masterminded by some South Westerners? Is it not true that even when a South Westerner is riding the popular crest of leadership, mudslinging and envy are orchestrated by South Westerners themselves? Is the South Westerner not himself a victim of economic illusions? To be endowed with natural resources without human industry will lead to no economic prosperity. The real economy is in the hands of petty traders like street hawkers, craftsmen, transportation. If the South West Elites do not encourage their masses morally and financially to invest in petty trade, the province will, in spite of its SONARA boom, face an Economic doom.

There is therefore need to create a cultural and developmental association whose functions respond to the day to day needs of its local communities. One which is non-partisan like a non-governmental organisation with networks that can promote the ebbing culture and stalled development of the Province. There must be a rational sale of land to its own natives no matter how small and cheap. It is the only guarantee of guarding posterity. According to Barrister Taku, less than 25% of land in Meme, Ndian and Fako is owned by the natives. Most of the land is not only in the hands of North Westerners but strange enough, in the hands of Francophones. Why does South West tolerate domination from Betis, Bassas and Bamis but are quick to reject leadership from the North West? The South Westerner must believe in himself, know his capacities and recognise his own shortcomings. If the South Westerner wants to remain a passive pedestrian on the highway while others who have the courage to fight for their rights are doing so, let him blame nobody. But let him not make strangers, the scapegoats of his own deficiency. We can bury all our squabbles and wrangles if only we admit that they exist and the need to bridge the divide is imperative. It is in this vein that the press and opinion leaders have a lofty mission.

Press

The Private Press has pursued a laudable mission of highlighting the Anglophone problem. It has successfully exported the Anglophone Liberation struggle to the National and International Arenas but it has failed to recognise the democratic values inherent in each individual when dealing with the Anglophone file.

The skill with which the written press has handled proponents of two or ten state has left much to be desired. And for anybody who has tried to carry the North West/South West doctrine to the village especially in the South West would agree that "Some over-zealous colleagues have twisted facts bordering on the North West/South West divide that the South West feels there's something sinister to hide". We all have one goal but using the means of nagging and howling, ranting and raving, intimidating and insulting will not get us to our goal. The Private Press is in danger of fanning the North West/South West divide like they considerably contributed in widening the gulf within the opposition parties. We need a press that can convince the individual completely. The press must live above partisan and tribal leanings if the goal of Anglophone Unity must be achieved. We need a responsible and mature press that transcends the cacophony of hero-worshiping and villain-bashing to accommodate the dissenting ideas and embark on the magnetism of cajoling and congregating instead of the policy of exclusion. Don't get it wrong. The press has a duty to castigate those ideas that are not in harmony with the welfare of the people.

The press being the fourth Power has the energy to mould public opinion and so each word that denigrates any NW/SW opinion leader's personality goes a long way to alienate part of a North West/South West community. Columnists and writers who have ventured to do mediating literature between North West/Southwest have sometimes betrayed their tribal instincts. This is a delicate field and one can only borrow a leaf from Dr. Munzu's rejoinder to Mr. Agbor Nkongho's letter in "Cameroon Post" or Cyprian Agbor's, reply to Lobe Kingsley letter in "The Messenger". They attacked issues not personalities. They criticised without sounding emotional. If our noble Press must maintain its credibility as the watchdog of a free society then it should remain the market place for ideas and leave the gallery of mudslinging to the vagaries of gutter journalism.

Time for North West/South West Dialogue

We need unity now even if we cannot attain uniformity. As I see it the Southern Cameroon Peoples Council (SCPC) has an arduous task ahead of it and that is why organised groups like SWELA, CAM, FREE West Cameroon Movement, Ambazonia, NOCUDA etc. must employ their well-grounded structures at the service of SCPC by acting as complimentary organs.

These organs must understand the triple mission SCPC Standing Committee now has in front of it. The AAC of 2 and 3 April 1993 in Mount Mary was not convened to settle the North West/South West Divide. It was convened to send home a message that there is an Anglophone problem which should be taken care of in any constitutional conference. Having transmitted this message and while it is being concretised and sensitisation missions are operating on the national and international levels, SCPC should now select members to form a small commission of equal representation of North Westerners and South Westerners to sit and discuss issues bordering on the North West/South West Divide. The aim of such a commission would be to frankly and fairly discuss these issues, study the preliminary federal constitution proposed by Elad, Munzu and Anyangwe, suggest amendments taking cognizance of the vertical (Francophone/Anglophone) and horizontal (North West/South West) problems that confront us. At the end of the exercise, a joint statement would be issued by the commission endorsing the amended Federal Constitution. In other words, the SCPC's triple mission is to carry foreign support, lobby national associations (Chiefs, Fons, Parliamentarians, Parties, Pressure groups) and furthermore bridge the North West/South West divide. SCPC's foreign role should be to project the Anglophone problem (marginalisation of Anglophones) while its introspective role is to probe into the Anglophone file (North West/South West issues). Both roles should be carried out diligently and concurrently. We may conquer international and national support but lose regional grounds if our house is not put in order before the next phase of the constitutional talks. Come to think of it, it is a blessing that the "Grand Debat" did not hold then otherwise Anglophones would have come in speaking different languages. Now is the time to exploit the regime's delay tactics to heal our own wounds. We need to be seen as having largely fulfilled these three requirements before we start "viewing that the AAC has exhausted its mandate, the "grand debat" having failed".

We need to methodically undertake these initiatives before we start taking supersonic flights into the orbit of "Action" and "zero option". We need to initiate a North West/South West dialogue where among other things there should be an elected, enlarged and broadly represented constituent assembly. Such a dialogue should create an atmosphere whereby while the North Westerner should tell himself that it will not happen again the South Westerner should now vow that it must never happen again. We may not achieve unanimity but we would achieve a Rainbow coalition that will give the North West/South West Divide a new impetus and a new perspective. We may not achieve unanimity because in our flock there are fatalists, career saboteurs, unrepentant extremists and perpetual agitators. With the Anglophone history in hindsight, there is a possibility that some Anglophones today are singing the Redemption song of Anglophone Liberation for their own personal end. The clash between Jua/Muna and Egbe Tabi/Nzou Ekangaki three decades ago lends credence to this.

At any time in our history, when leadership begins to emerge among Anglophones as it is today, overzealousness, egocentric impulses, personality clashes, veiled parochial leanings and eventual betrayal gets into play. As a former member of the Standing Committee of the SCPC, I dare say that the SCPC has struck a match in corners where there was darkness. Let it be given the time to carry the light around. I have always believed that if SCPC fails in its triple mission today it will not be so much due to the insensitivity and intransigence of the status quo. It will be due to the ripples of betrayal and the vicious process of auto intoxication that have often characterised the bedrock of any Anglophone struggle. God Forbid!!! Our history today is full of giants with clay feet who have not only left indelible footprints of treachery on the sands of time but have persistently kow-towed to the cosmetic pleasures of a fool's paradise. What we need tomorrow is a pantheon full of patriotic iconoclasts whose hearts should be throbbing to the rhythm of Ngom Jua's credo and whose souls should be stirred by the legacy of Monyongo Kale's vision. For the Cameroonian flowers of tomorrow to blossom with democratic radiance and linguistic diversity, the Anglophone bees of today must carry with hurried slowness but determined sureness the federal pollen to all the cardinal points of our triangular garden. To be federated or not to be?-that is the national question that now occupies the front page of the Anglophone File.

CHAPTER FIVE

WHY WE NEED A TWO BY (X) STATE FEDERATION

The common denominator between the Southwest and the Northwest Provinces is that they both stand for a Federation. A ten state Federation emphasises Provincial Protection, while a two state federation emphasises state of Regional Sovereignty. The magic numbers of two and ten have put the North westerner and South westerner at daggers drawn as if any of the formulas has been bought by the government yet. We have been so divided along the lines of two and ten that we refuse to see the issues involved and the risks concerned. Just as we have painted a wholly divided so have we given a false impression that a person who believes in the two state federations must be a north westerner or a south westerner or a southwest "lunatic". We have been so concerned with labels and tags that we pay no attention to the fact that there is a crucial content which is that there is a vertical dichotomy between Anglophones and Francophone and a horizontal schism between northwest and southwest.

Any constitution that embarks on a solely ten state arrangement without an institutionalised umbrella over the Northwest and Southwest provinces would be like a house with a solid foundation but without a good roof.

Any constitution that embarks on a solely two state arrangement (west Cameroon/East Cameroon), with the proviso that internal matters between the Anglophone brother is like a house with a strong roof but without a solid foundation.

We need a constitution that concurrently handles the Anglophone/Francophone problem and the Northwest/Southwest problems. A constitution that does not lay emphasis on posts and personalities but on opportunities and issues.

The EMA Constitution

Having gone through most of the draft constitutions presented by individuals and organisations, one cannot help but use the Draft Federation Constitution proposed by Elad, Munzu and Anyangwe (EMA) as the working document. It is a document that both attain that goal of national character and the objective of regional development. No other document so far has eloquently expressed and contained a two tier of federation (Vertical and horizontal levels) like the EMA constitution. It is therefore fallacious to propagate the philosophy that the EMA constitution stands for two states as against four, ten, fifteen states as propounded by other organisations. The document indeed is flexible to any number of states that the people of Cameroon would so desire; with the sole difference that the people of Southern Cameroons (West Cameroon) like those of La Republique du Cameroon (East Cameroun) would on sovereign basis prescribe the number of states (autonomous provinces) within their territories. The constitution already provides Provincial autonomy between the two provinces of Northwest and Southwest (it is up to the various inhabitants to maintain and secure their financial and administrative autonomy) under the umbrella of a West Cameroon State.

The document makes provision for a distinct identity and bicultural nature of two people who came into political union in 1961 which forms the basis of a historical legality and provision for the fulfilment of the aspirations of the masses within the entire country toward decentralisation, devotion and decongestion of power to the periphery which forms the basis of a socio-political reality. Any document worth its salt must take cognisance of the historical legality and socio-political reality of the Cameroonian people.

Proponents of a ten state Federation have religiously borrowed their phenomenon possibly from the Nigerian experience. Let it be made clear that while Nigeria operates on a monolingual background that permits a common legal, educational and ex-cultural system throughout the nation, Cameroon operates on a bilingual and bicultural level that produces two parallel legal, educational and ex-cultural systems. No matter how African anybody wants to feel, the blatant truth about African politics is that its policies are still tele-guided by the ingredients of our foreign languages. Because Cameroon finds herself in this dual situation, the conflict of the Anglophones and Francophone would be omnipresent except the former allow themselves to be swallowed like Anglophone Jonases in the belly of the Francophone whale. The two foreign systems (English and French) are the real custodians of power and decision making in Cameroon and any loose allowance for a ten state Federation would give a free visa to France to totally assimilate the weak and timid John Bullism in the Anglophone territory of Cameroon.

A Matter of Values

One of the expectations of the ten states Federation is that it will allow for indigenous Governors to be elected as it is in the EMA constitution. Yet in a loose arrangement of ten states, no one would be surprised if the President insisted on appointing Governors who are indigenes of the area. That defeats the purpose of administrative autonomy, for the Governor would not be responsible to the people but his master that appointed him. Lastly, the loose arrangement of ten states denigrates the Southern Cameroons sovereignty into mere Provinces or states. Plagued by a history of treachery, traumatised by an element of domination, the ten state proponent is losing his own personality and reducing his own statehood to simple provincial expressions. As we made our way through the labyrinth of our fragmented past let us not lose sight of the graceful values that unite us toward a glorious future. We are a nation born out of the complexities of colonialism, bred against the tides of cultural Assimilation but prepared today to grow within a distinct heritage of a linguistic ancestry. Equal status was achieved in 1961 in an arrangement where our sovereignty was equal to another sovereignty. How do we move from a 1:1 relationship to clamour for a 2:8 arrangement? According to Dr. Carlson Anyangwe, "Southern Cameroonians are unquestionably a people whose own distinctiveness is undeniable. There is and can be no dispute that our British derived culture has a separate, long and distinct history. That culture is in present danger of disappearing". We must therefore capitalise on what unites and strengthens us as a free people not highlight what divides and weakens us like a conquered people. This is the mission of the two by (x) state constitution that Elad, Munzu and Anyangwe propose to the Cameroon people in general and to the

Anglophones in particular. While we all have a right to fight to personal positions and provincial protections, our main drive should be to restore our declining Anglo-Saxon values. We are talking about our educational system that has been eroded in our Technical, Teachers Training Centres, Secondary and even Higher Education. If our students can stand together for an Anglo-Saxon University and we all stood for the creation of an Examinations Board, why can't we stand together as Anglophones?

We are talking about our territorial integrity that is being invaded and our cultural existence not being expressed externally. If we could stand together for the clamour to be a member of Commonwealth why can't we stand together as Anglophones?

We are talking about the role of the military in a sane and democratic society; in the old West Cameroon days; the policemen meant the representative and guardian of the city-the symbol of human civilisation. A policeman was politeness, for politeness carries the elegance of a steward. Today not only have the police degenerated into a squadron of blood suckers, not only are we acquainted with disorderly gendarme brutality; we are now helpless victims of lawless military bestiality. For record purposes, the first gendarme assault on West Cameroon soil was carried out on September 14, 1962 in Nkambe by a certain gendarme called Jean Roumain Amougou. He beat up two innocent civilians mercilessly and when questioned he said gendarmes were above the law and he believed in the French military system of enforcing discipline. If we could all heed to CAM's Solidarity Call of 11 August 1993, why can't we stand together as Anglophones?

We are talking of a system of accountability with a main economic data showing social, economic and financial statistics that was specific and could be checked by an Auditor. If we all condemned the Messi Messi scandal, the CAM GAZ SCTM and CELUCAM affairs, why can't we stand together as Anglophones? We are talking about a healthy Environment with a clean water supply and adequate garbage disposal measures reminiscent of the days of the West Cameroonian Sanitary Inspectors. If we unanimously elected Yaounde, the Garbage City of the year, why can't we stand together as Anglophones? As Peter Nsanda Eba once wrote "we must protect the values which those in my generation and older generation were raised up in. A lot of these values have been eroded, and it has been the hopes and wishes that our generation will die off, so that the future generations can grow up in mediocrity. We must unite to ensure the continuity of these values in future generations".

Unity in Concept

Yes the West Cameroon of 1961 – 1972 was not a Paradise and so some have contested the EMA document as a return to the horrors and terrors of an evil system and a revisit of the Kangaroo that jumps into its mother's pouch in times of danger. It must be made clear here the EMA's stand on 1961 is basically for historical legality but its structures, modalities in fact its modus operandi is in harmony with the socio-political realities from the document could be made here. In the 1961 constitution, the President had the full powers to appoint the Prime Minister according to his whims and caprices only for the Parliament to rubber stamp it, the EMA constitution provides for the appointment of a Prime Minister by the President based on a suggestion of the State Executive Council. In other words the President only rubber stamps what the people (state executive council) have already decided.

In the 1961 constitution, the Prime Minister had total powers over the entire West Cameroon territory within an infinite period and all the P.M.'s came from the North West Province.

The EMA constitution limits the Prime Minister's function to "over-seeing" the territory and representing his state in state matters (like night watch of Territorial invasion and assimilation), has a specific term of office which alternates between the Provinces.

The 1961 arrangement did not provide for elected Governors and Local Council representatives as found in the EMA constitution. There was no principle in the 1961 constitution guiding the law of Derivation and Revenue Distribution and so the Southwest became the milking cow of the country. Without pride or prejudice, without rage or rancour but in good faith and in good will let every Cameroonian in general and every Anglophone in particular read the EMA draft Federation Constitution and make recommendations. The document may have flaws but should be the working document. One contesting factor that comes against the EMA constitution especially among some South westerners is the eligibility of the Provincial Governors. A clause that stipulates that a Governor would be elected from (...) and from non-natives who have spent a number of years in the Province is ridiculous. Not only does it entertain a repeat of the non-native syndrome but deprives the real native of freely electing their own "sons of the soil". Instead of a non-native occupying the highest office of a province, the privileges and rights of non-natives would be taken care of by the election of a percentage composition in the provincial assemblies, Provincial Executive Council and Local Government areas. This argument should be given serious thought. The need to accommodate views from Anglophones to the Draft Federal Constitution is extremely vital so that the Liberation of Anglophones does not lead to the enslavement of any of the Provinces in the West Cameroon territory.

That SWELA had taken a stand on a ten state Federation since 1991 is nothing new; that some Chiefs of the Southwest took a ten state stand on 10 April 1993 is nothing new; that the LDP had taken a ten state stand then endorsed the EMA document is nothing new; that the NDP had taken a four state stand then endorsed the EMA document is nothing new; that the CRP has taken a stand on ten states is nothing new; that CAM had taken a two state stand then endorsed the EMA document is nothing new; that the AAC has endorsed the EMA document is nothing new and that the SDF party finally took a stand on Federation is nothing new. What is new in the history of southern Cameroons is that all Anglophones (pressure groups and parties) have like one people agreed on a unique concept-the concept of Federalism as against the concept of Unilateralism. This is different from the 1961 plebiscite decision that threw Anglophones apart between the concept of Reunification with Cameroon and the concept of Integration with Nigeria. This is a new found Unity. If we are so united in the concept of Federalism, why do we allow ourselves to be manipulated by the magical numbers of two and ten? Have we even succeeded in getting across the real concept of Federalism yet? Why do we spend atoms of energy against ourselves? - Energy that could be mustered for the concept of Federalism to be accepted. Why do we spend iota of intelligence destroying our case and cause? - Intelligence that could be harnessed to liberate the Anglophones and protect our provincial peculiarities. Why do we spend valuable time inviting a battalion of soldiers against our own people?

Come to think of it, the Francophone Administration does not know the art of negotiation. Original demands in the Bamenda Conference of June 1961 which include separate Government; Capital to Douala, bicameral Federal Legislature, ceremonial not executive Head of State, a Governor as Head of each state with Prime Minister, different legal systems etc. made by the Southern Cameroonian delegation to the negotiation table in Foumban July 1961 were simply rejected for many reasons among them:-

(1) The Southern Cameroonians were hyper-motivated by jingoistic zeal and naive faith in their Francophone "brothers". While the banner in the hall carried a pompous dictum in English of "How nice it is to meet our brothers" the French equivalent was simply "Vive le Cameroun Unifie".

(2) The Bamenda proposals limited Presidential powers and Ahidjo did not want a diminution of his authority and power.

(3) The over-optimistic but patriotic Bamenda proposals were whittled down since Yaounde as usual, had her own plans. The proposals of Bamenda were simply ignored and Ahidjo brought out his own document which some members of the Southern Cameroonian delegation were seeing for the first time on the morning of the opening ceremony. Indeed the leader of opposition requested that he be allowed time to study the document. The Southern Cameroonian delegation was given three days to study Ahidjo's document (we were given 15 days to study Owona's).

(4) In the face of Ahidjo's Ruritanian ruse and Machiavellian machinations, the southern Cameroon delegation was shy at making its disapproval heard and dejection heard. Instead its leaders (Foncha, Endeley) were carried in the hysteria of home coming and in the frenzy of fraternal union as they pontificated on pious patriotic platitudes and sterile sycophantic sermons – all in the name of peace; in the name of unity.

(5) The conference ended on the promise that both delegations (Southern Cameroon & La

Republique du Cameroun) would meet later to develop on the constitution. To every one's surprise Ahidjo broke the promise, got the national assembly to adopt the shoddy constitution which the promulgated into law without consulting the Southern Cameroons House of Assembly; that is what became the Federal Constitution on October 1, 1961. What came out of Foumban therefore was nothing but the French plans for the then Federal Republic of Cameroon.

Even if the ten state Federation is accepted today like Foncha's clamour for Reunification with French Cameroon was accepted yesterday and the two by (x) state Federation is ignored today like P. M Kale's third option was ignored yesterday, the story will be told that the hurricane of discordant opinions swept away the mustard seed of Anglophone Unity. It should not happen. If Fon Achirimbi II said yesterday that to go with Nigeria will be like drowning in water and to go with French Cameroons is like praying with our eyes closed and to stand for a two by (x) state Federation is like praying with our eyes opened – in this case you watch and pray at the same time. In the search for Southern Cameroons self-determination in Nigeria, the Richards constitution was replaced by the Macpherson constitution in 1951. The Macpherson constitution provided bedrock for the southern Cameroon people. The Macpherson Constitution recognised the need for survival of Anglophones in Cameroon.

As the Macpherson constitution provided the "great leap" for the crystallisation of political aspirations for Southern Cameroon leaders, so does the EMA constitution provide the "great hope" for the manifestation of societal opportunities for the Anglophone people.

Dedication to the Unborn

Today, we are acting in defence of the unborn because we are living on borrowed time. We owe a whole generation that has been saddled with a burden of economic debts and has been passed the mantle of moral mediocrity, the supreme price of self-abnegation. Imbued with academic knowledge, traditional wisdom, collective experience and intrinsic foresight, we cannot afford to bring our nation to her stomach now that she is already on her knees. The question of leadership rotates around us – We, who still possess some vestiges of humane values and respect for human civilisation. Does the rising power and popularity of Anglophone leadership not ring a bell to you? It does to me. It rings a bell that the democratisation process in Cameroon can only be delayed, it can never be denied. It rings a bell that though we all climbed the Mount Mary Mountain top together some of us sometimes descend the valley of despair and still grope in the wilderness of mutual suspicion. But even though our feet are weary and our minds worried, our eyes have seen the promised land of Federalism and we shall all get there sooner than later. Come along, the journey has just begun. We shall walk behind a leader who will not only diligently guide and guard the ninety-nine sheep but patiently and meticulously go in search of the lost one. And so the youths of today must brace themselves for such leadership, as the old are making their onward march to their last homes. As the leadership in the West revolves around the children of the post World War era so the leadership in Africa must now revolve around the children of the post-independent era.

Last CREDO

To have a Federation that will be a happy place to live in and that is the envy of the world would not be without obstacles but let us borrow Augustine Ngom Jua's credo which reads "I believe that the future holds bright prospects for the Federated State of West Cameroon in particular, and the Federal Republic in general, and that with a Government imbued with foresight and lofty ideals, animated by a spirit of selflessness and fired with imagination to put the nation and its citizens above all else, we shall overcome all obstacles" let us keep the credo alive.

FRAGMENTS OF UNITY

(To every son and daughter of the South West)

CHAPTER ONE

OUR GEOGRAPHY

The South West Province was born from the 1972 decree that transferred the Federal Republic of Cameroon to the United Republic of Cameroon. Mount Fako imposes her towering height of 4095m over the four divisions that make up the Province. The four Divisions include FAKO with headquarters in Limbe and other towns including Buea, Tiko and Muyuka; MEME with headquarters in Kumba and other towns including Tombel, Nguti and Bangem, MANYU with headquarters in Mamfe and other towns including Akwaya, Fontem and Eyumojock; NDIAN with headquarters in Mundemba and other towns including Bamusso, Ekondo Titi, Kombo Abedimo, Kombo Itindi, Isangele and Idabato. (At the time of writing of this book in 1992, the divisions of Kupe Mwanenguba and Lebialem had not been created).

The main ethnic groups in the Province are the Bima, Ngolo, Bakossi, Balue, Nweh, Bayang, Ejagham, Bakundu, Balondo, Bafaw, Bakweri etc. Bounded on the East by the Littoral and Western Provinces, on the West by the Federal Republic of Nigeria, on the North by the North West Province, and on the South by the

145

Atlantic Ocean, the South West Province has a land area of 27,520 square km.

The physical features of the province range from the swampy and marshy coastline, through numerous volcanic lakes to the main vegetation cover which is the equatorial forest.

With high temperatures and heavy rain falls, the province experiences a rich harvest of subsistence and cash crops that have made her the bee hive of economic activities in the country. Although the plethora of industries and the diversity of touristic sites serve as bait to foreigners and tourists, the transport and communication infrastructures make the province a caricature of balanced development.

The province prides herself with giant industries like CDC, PAMOL, PLANTECAM, etc. which without political meddling can generate income to the inhabitants and provide employment to the local citizens. The presence of these industries however has shifted emphasis from the small and medium size enterprises that call for mass participation and diversified labour.

Petty trades and Associations like Cooperatives and Farmers banks have become the monopoly of aliens since the South Westerner would rather get dissatisfied salary from a white collar job than get a job that would make him more of a servant than a master.

In a province where Rubber, Banana, Oil and Tea are produced, a census of the average labourer roll reveals that the South Westerner is in the minority and when we know that most industrial policies demand that the top class must rise from the ranks of the industry, we are not surprised why even at the top echelon we find ourselves wanting. It is the "water-boy" that may become the Manager tomorrow, it is the "rubber tapper" that may be the boss the following day; everything being equal, all it takes is patience, endurance and hard work to climb the top rungs of the industrial ladder. The hawkers who loiter on our streets with commodities on their heads, the petty traders who spend hours in their stores, the indefatigable mobile restaurant women, the butchers and taxi men are those who have the economy in their hands at the end of the day. With their wealth, they head sporting and religious associations in the province thereby boosting not only their economic stand but more their social status. We are all witnesses to the fact that non-natives have held even our petty and medium size enterprises hostage. They have invested in our land, they have the labour and they are stashing away the capital. This has nothing to do with the colonial invasion of Africa, for colonialism was a historical fact with a necessary evil. It has something to do with the cultural servitude of the Province for the dependence syndrome have been the hallmark of the South Westerner especially in fields that demand labour and capital. Armed with this mentality of dependence and equipped with this culture of brazen arrogance, the South West has in the wake lost the umbrella factory in Moliwe. With the giant industries only standing erect as white elephants, the South Westerner must go down to his economic roots and occupy those "working-class" or blue collar jobs that will make him sweat and toil but that will leave him with a swollen coffer and a satisfied heat. When the 20th May Referendum train passed in 1972 sounding the trumpet of political chicanery, the Tiko and Besong Abang Airports developed into the Siberia of Transport Infrastructure. The river port of Mamfe, deep sea port of Bota and creek port in Tiko now look back in anger at the days when they surrendered their economic virginity to the lascivious and lecherous merchants who made the cities not only bustling but rendered the economy lucrative. But that was the pre-72 years. The ports now lie beneath the waves like Yoke Hydro Electric Power, like Mbanga-Kumba Railway, like a plane anchored to the bottom of the sea.

And they said "let there be light" and there was light even with its draconian electricity bill, electricity is still a rare commodity in the rural areas and water may be found everywhere yet there is still none to drink. The few public taps found on the streets have become battle fields for young children who must queue up in a circle and jostle around for those precious drops of water. Where water does not flow from the public taps, the citizens depend on streams and rivers thereby defying the ambitions slogan of "Health by the year 2000". While some citizens like in Ekondo Titi cannot understand government's policy of not providing them with water or roads, those in Buea do not take it lying low. A few months ago, a group of women marched to the Governor's office in Buea to protest against the closure of taps in the jurisdiction. Water flushed from the taps the next day. With hopes almost lost for inter urban roads especially between Kumba-Mamfe and Kumba-Ndian; the focus today is on feeder roads. Those roads provide the urbanities with daily meals; but the roads neither exist thereby rendering the areas enclave or where they do exists, they are inaccessible thereby linking the prices of basic subsistence crops brought to the market. When the infighting among political barons and witch-hunting among the people's representative will be over, when the sun of a new political order will rise, government's priority will be on transport infrastructure, for roads are the vehicles of development. The Tombel-Nyassoso-Bangem road, the Toko-Madie Ngolo road, all groan and moan for repairs as the entrails of these villages are bursting with foodstuff waiting to be delivered to Kumba, Buea, Ndian and Mamfe, and also to the country's economic and administrative capitals whose gluttonous appetites for local food is insatiable. Even though FONADER Produce Marketing Board have not been replaced with a Farmer's Bank "Credit Agricole" the farmers will never give up for 85% of the population relies on the soil not for its black gold but the green gold that has made agriculture the main-stay of the province. Not even the fall in price of cocoa and coffee will discourage them for the prices will rise and local industries will be built to process our own products and export some to those who need them. For the advent of SOWEDA means the requiem to bureaucracy. The Development Authority would tackle those projects that employ a sizeable number of the wretched of the province, those projects that can consume the blue-collared and provide opportunities to the creative talents: SOWEDA would be more practical than idealistic letting her rhetoric fall like hailstones on the ground of reality.

And the SOWEDANS would not be career politicians fighting for higher post or struggling to maintain a high one. They would be seasoned administrators committed to the task of development and seeing into the economic security of the cream and the scum. We have not lost all. Our communication network still looms large over the horizon. Radio Buea has survived the tides of poor communication infrastructures. She yearns to be better than some of her new brides in other provinces. The T.V. Operation has gone provincial but for Ndian or specifically Mundemba whose CRTV images remain blurred or non-existent at all. Yet the division needs a powerful TV antenna given its strategic position around the borders and its propensity for borrowed culture from Nigerian neighbours. People often identify themselves with the culture they are exposed to. As the race for appropriate not advanced technology continues, our technical schools must have a lot of input in practical technology. Not just the maintenance and repairs of computers. TV and high technology are important but the basic repairs and assembly of cars, telephone and locally fabricated items should be the main focus. Ombe shall rise from slumber. The trade centres will lift their bushels on the economic table. Technology will be a main preoccupation for the technical students as the secondary school graduates look forward to the University of Buea. Maybe someday the graduates would be told that going out of the university without the university getting in to you is half-baked education. They would graduate with an eye not only for government jobs but for private enterprises for government cannot absorb all the citizens. The government must therefore make privatisation less complicated through the overhauling of policies affecting small and medium size enterprises and the reduction of revenue taxes and prices of business licenses. These factors have stifled creative initiatives. Talents must be exposed in the cultural, social, economic and political domains. Incentives will help expose these talents to national aspirations and international challenges. And the people of the province will be proud and that will make this good old country proud. Then the history of their leaders will be told, partly to inform the world that the leadership vacuum is a new phenomenon and purely to assert the province as a cradle of leadership.

Hopefully the young in whose hands the destiny of the province lies may draw inspiration from the heroes of yesterdays and correct the mistakes that would turn our new leaders into veritable political icons. Here then is the pantheon of the actors whose political acumen carved for the south west a respectable and enviable place in the political theatre of our patrimony.

CHAPTER TWO

YESTERDAY'S HEROES – THE CRADLE OF SOUTH WEST

Leadership: Dr. Emmanuel Mbella Liffafe Endeley

Dr. Emmanuel Mbella Liffafe Endeley was born on April 10th 1916 at Buea. He was educated at the Roman Catholic Mission School Bonjongo and at the Government Secondary School of Medicine and after his graduation he was assigned to Lagos but was dismissed in 1946 for alleged medical misconduct. In 1947, when in Buea he became the Secretary of the C.D.C. Worker's Union. In 1950, his name was restored to the medical register. He helped to form the CNF and in 1951 he was elected to the Nigerian Federal Assembly in Lagos representing the Southern Cameroons. He founded the KNC and was the first Premier of Southern Cameroons. He was defeated in 1959 when he campaigned for integration with Nigeria. He is a well-seasoned politician. In 1960, he helped form the Cameroon Peoples' National Congress (CPNC). He died on June 29 1988 (Victor Ngoh "Cameroon-A Hundred Years of History").

It would be an insult to Historians of Dr. Victor Ngoh's calibre if the historical strides that veteran politicians took were to be mentioned here. But this chapter only aims at revealing the fact that the South West Province has never had a leadership vacuum. Instead the province has been the Bethlehem of Cameroonian Politics producing fiery and fire brand orators on one hand and cautions and moderate leaders on the other hand. It is this blend of modernisation and radicalism that has characterised south west leadership although at one time the pendulum has been oscillating from an extreme to another. Dr. Endeley was one of those fiery orators whose personality traits however brought in a lot of controversy. His political astuteness was readily translated as arrogance and his towering height cowed down the "Lilliputians" that stood on his way as opponents.

Fale Wache (Editor of *Cameroon Life*) remarked that Endeley tended to be brash, scornful, supercilious and downright contemptuous of the other politicians. Yet I believe that when an academic giant meddles with opponents whose vision for the future is myopic, the giant's desert of foresight and inner vision are transformed to an oasis of aggression. Endeley's opponents were extremely naïve and had the tragic flaw of believing in the goodness of man and in the piety of human nature. A slogan like "How nice it is to meet our brothers again" that hung over the hall that was to decide the fate of the delicate union between

Anglophones and Francophones was to say the least puerile. In the rough and tumble game of politics it may be fair-play in principle but it is the winner-take-it all in practice. Fale Wache goes ahead to vividly describe three outstanding stories that made Endeley an arrogant politician. Once on a visit to the Mamfe area, Endeley boasted to the people there that whatever they did, they could never achieve the intellectual brilliance and prowess of the Bakweri, epitomised of course by him Endeley. Secondly, though a Prince (some even said heir apparent) of the Buea Endeley dynasty, EML Endeley is reported to have treated the extremely aristocratic Fon of Bali, Galega I, with levity. One version holds that on a trip to London after alighting from the plane, he asked the Fon to carry his bag.

Lastly another story tells us Endeley who told a rally that if the people did not vote him, then the stones and trees of Fako Mountain were sure to vote for him.

For any politician at this time to throw his academic and abrasive qualities in front of his political career was tantamount to political suicide. As educated as Endeley was he failed to channel his academic prowess to his advantages; and through rhetoric he alienated himself from the warmth of the masses – he needed these masses for the votes. Even in the heat of an election campaign; Endeley refused to speak to the Fons in the language they understood (pidgin) with the excuse that "I apologise to the Fons that I cannot speak in any other way". That has been the undoing of the South West politician - his inability to communicate with the grass-root. Any leader who adamantly stays on the roof of rhetoric without building a solid foundation of mass mobilisation will be reduced to a pure juggler in the comedy of politics. For not only did Endeley consider his contemporaries are mere intellectual minions but he saw them as villagers and outright natives. Endeley is alleged to have been indecisive. Although he took a stand on integrating with Nigeria, he abandoned it, requested that together with the KNDP, they should pressurise the United Nations to include an option that never materialised. It is this swinging attitude of arrogance, indecision and fence-sitting that virtually marred Endeley's political career.

Yet who will forget his steadfastness and adroitness when he stood his grounds? The Limbe oil pipeline is one of those milestones that has dwarfed Endeley's flaw and brought him into the Hall of Fame. The flame of Endeley stopped sparkling on June 1988. When Barrister Taku Charles of Buea was asked to make his comments on Endeley he made the following remarks:

- I will decline to judge Dr. E.M.L Endeley in the light of a Baweri leader because his greatest aspiration was to become a National Leader and he succeeded.

- He was a spokesman of the people in the oppressive days of the First Republic and in most instances his voice was heard; the difficulties notwithstanding.

- He encountered and animated the spirit of oneness and democracy in Cameroon.

The legacy of Endeley's ideology lingers on, twisted by the tides of time and shifted by the sands of fate.

Paul Monyongo Kale

If there was one leader that was capable of mellowing down the flame of radicalism with the water of modernisation, it was indeed P.M. Kale. Born on March 20, 1910 in Buea, at a time when politics belonged to extremist P.M. Kale chose the middle of the road to steer an objective course that would bring warning ideologies to a compromise. P.M. Kale was first and foremost a scholar who left Buea on April 1935 for the purpose of pursing further studies in Fourah Bay College, Sierra Leone but to quote him "the wind of fate dropped me in Lagos Nigeria where I sojourned for well over seventeen years and abandoned the idea of going to Sierra Leone".

In Nigeria, he was inspired by the writings of Azikiwe and became not only a writer (he wrote "Brief

History of the Bakweri", "CYL Newsletter" and Political Evolution in the Cameroons") but also became a budding politician. In 1940 Kale and his cousin EML Endeley founded the Cameroons Youth League (CYL) a pressure group whose objective was to arouse National consciousness of British Cameroonians as well as to seek a recognised status for Southern Cameroons. In 1953 Kale abandoned the CYL to form the Kamerun People's Party (KPP) together with N.N. Mbile. In 1959 he formed the Kamerun United Party (KUP) that stood midway between the possibility of burning ourselves in "fire" by joining French Cameroons or drowning ourselves in "water" by integrating to the Republic of Nigeria. P.M. Kale opted for a third alternative of an independent Southern Cameroon. But even though Kale warned the Secretary General that the Kamerun United Party would do nothing short of boycotting the Plebiscite if Britain and the United Nation refused to include a third alternative at the Plebiscite on 11th February, 1961, the United Nation still went ahead with the two options of either integrating with Nigeria or unifying with Cameroon. According to Kale, the Plebiscite question was tantamount to dictatorship or tyranny by the British who were forcing emancipated Cameroonians politically and otherwise to accept living under the government of the Cameroon Republic and the Federation of Nigeria. Kale wanted an independent southern Cameroons with membership in the Common-Wealth. But in the eyes of the British, the population of the southern Cameroon was too small to stand on its own and in the minds of the British economists the Southern Cameroon was not economically viable to make up an independent geographical entity.

Apart from this, Kale's alliance with Dr. Nnamdi Azikiwe's party – National Council of Nigeria and the Cameroons (NCNC) was a political flaw. This was because the NCNC was dominated by the Ibos. And the Ibos were known to have treated Cameroonians with spite socially and economically, they had also occupied the petty commerce and civil service in the Southern Cameroon. This Ibo hegemony brought fears and suspicion among the southern Cameroonians, and they looked at such an alliance as a threat to their chances of advancement in the southern Cameroons. Thus because of the Ibo-phobia and British recalcitrance to access southern Cameroon per se, Kale's third option died a natural death. That's why today some political activities still hold Britain responsible for the predicament of southern (West) Cameroons. While France was acting as a mentor and guide to East Cameroon in the Foumban Conference, Britain in her characteristic way left southern Cameroon to her own device. Even the plebiscite question of "Do you wish to achieve INDEPENDENCE" by joining the independent … beats my imagination. How can a politically ambitious area seek independence by being annexed to another independent country? The fear for the Ibo hegemony by southern Cameroonians was rooted deeply in the psyche of inferiority complex for today the Ibos may not be raping our women but they are dating them, they may not be forcing their articles on us, but they are selling them to us and they are still having the petty commerce in their hands. Three decades after, the South West economy is still being lulled on the laps of the overzealous and indigenous Ibos. Has time not proved Kale's detractors wrong? On the 10th of January 1962, P.M. Kale was appointed speaker of the west Cameroon House of assembly. Before this appointment Kale was seen at a leader without a tribal or nepotic affinity, for though a cousin of Dr. EML Endeley they rarely saw eye to eye in politics because of ideological clashes. Kale was not a passenger on board the rocky boat of "Graffi/Coast" divide. In fact this is what Foncha had to say of him, during his (Kale) appointment as Speaker of West Cameroon House of Assembly. Courtesy of Cameroon Life Oct. 90.

"He (Kale) is a man of normal behaviour, he has no place to let his anger show out, and where, when he feels that he should let out his anger, he shrank and only did so when he was forced to. He wears a smiling face and cheerful spirit all the time. Under the circumstances which our political evolution has brought us, we can find no more suited person to be the speaker than this honourable person". Then, N. N. Mbile said "If I may suggest that I think is better for Mr. Kale, I will recommend that Mr. Kale is more suited to be an Ambassador somewhere. Mr. Kale, as I earlier said, has worked with me for years and I know his qualities. One of his qualities is that He is a First Class Diplomat".

Unfortunately, P.M. Kale did not live long to honour his imminent diplomatic career for his calibre and charisma were snatched by cold hands of death on August 22, 1966. Kale died and took with him the charm of an objective moderator and the courage of a cautious master planner. After reading through his book "The Political Evolution of the Cameroons" that was posthumously published, one would not help but admire the dream Kale had for Cameroon. He warned that for the English and French cultures to co-exist there must be Unity in Diversity. He said emphasis should be laid on the numerical population of the two cultures with a view to reviving the African original cultures and way of life. The political ideology and prophetic writings of P.M. Kale are a living memorial to the vision, the passion and the faith of a man whose message will never die.

Samson Adeoye George

Born in Mamfe on November 20, 1922, S.A. George grew up with the disadvantage of a child of two worlds (Nigeria and Cameroon) which nonetheless helped S.A. George sail across the turbulent seas of southern Cameroonian politics. His father, Henry George, was a Yoruba and his mother was from Mamfe. He did his education in Mamfe, Lagos and Port Harcourt. He worked with the Post and Telecommunications Department in Lagos before becoming a freelance journalist. He was a prominent member of the Zikist Vanguard and an active trade unionist in Nigeria. He was, at one time, the Secretary General of the Cameroons Youth League, (CYL). He was one of the "Original Thirteen" elected to the eastern House of Assembly, Nigeria and was also a member of the Nigerian House of Representatives. He advocated the reunification between the British and French Cameroons and he outlined his ideas in this "Kamerun Unification: Being a Discussion of a 7 Point-solution of the Unification Problem". He died in a London Hospital on October 10th, 1956 (Victor Julius Ngoh, "Constitutional Developments in Southern Cameroons 1946 – 1961).

History finds it difficult to record the achievements of young S.A. George for his political career was nipped in its prime by the cold hands of death. Nonetheless what cannot be got from the pages of history can be got from the experiences of historians. And so the mention of the name S.A. George to those who saw this fiery orator brings lively memories of a gentleman who had all that it took to be a man of the people. At the tender age of twenty-three, and as a worker with the Post and 'telecommunication Department in Lagos, S.A. George led the all first Nigerian strike at Enugu. Ripples of this Goliath task spread across Nigeria and made headlines in the Press. Inspired by Azikiwe's pan-Africanist views, S.A. George became his private secretary and blended his journalistic prowess with his inborn leadership qualities. He was a calm learner, frank and a brilliant orator. His glib-tongue could sway his opponents to his camp and it is only the likes of Motomby Woleta that could match his eloquence.

According to an interview granted me by Pa Atabong (Secretary General of Mundemba Rural Council) S.A. George was everybody's idol, and he (Pa Atabong) was the 'small' of S.A. George in the school days of Mamfe Government School. Showing a picture of S.A. George sent to him a week before his (S.A. George) death in London, Pa Atabong reveals with emotions the path that his mentor had prepared for the then West Cameroon. Bold and confident in his endeavours, S.A. George was the first to move the motion on "Benevolent Neutrality" in 1953 thereby giving rise to Party Politics. Prior to this the West Cameroonian politicians went to parliament as a block. He was instrumental in the success of Foncha's party and strange enough though his father was Yoruba, he wanted West Cameroon to secede from Nigeria and eventually stand on her own. Pa Atabong revealed with tears the circumstances that surrounded S.A. George's death (alleged poison and the strongly worded dismissal letter as Minister of Works written to him by EML Endeley and which he read on his sick bed. His doctor had advised that anything that could upset S.A. George should be avoided). There was one factor that S.A. George and Motomby Woleta had that distinguished them from EML Endeley and N.N. Mbile – Tolerance. S.A George could accommodate dissenting views and reconcile when the heat of arguments was over. He regarded disagreements as a necessary ingredient in the process of Democracy. This was different from the vendetta attitudes that N.N. Mbile and EML Endeley had toward their opponents. They were unable to stomach bitterness and challenges and easily fell prey to the cronies of sycophancy. S.A. George distinguished himself from the haughtiness of South West leaders who arrogate to themselves the divine rights of lording their ideas over everybody's. It is not so much the presence of S.A. George that we miss; it is the absence of his political will and democratic commitment that we regret.

Nerius Namaso Mbile

This is the last of the Titans who survived the battle of reunification, braved the war of Ahidjo's One Man Show, and weathered the storm of the New Deal. He was born on April 4, 1923 in Lipenja. He did his primary education in Kumba and his post primary education in Eastern Nigeria. He was one time a member of the NCNC, Secretary General of the CDC Workers' Union and later its President. He was also the Secretary General of the CNF and later KUNC. He was one of the "Original Thirteen" Elected in 1951 from southern Cameroons to the Eastern House of Assembly, Nigeria. He was instrumental in the formation of the KPP in 1953 and was its Deputy leader. He was a Minister in the first ministerial government in southern Cameroons. He was Deputy Leader of the CPNC and campaigned for association with Nigeria. He was Minister of works (1965 – 67), Minister of Lands and Surveys in 1968 and Secretary of State for Primary Education from 1969 - 1972 (Victor Julius Ngo "Constitutional Development in Southern Cameroons 1946 – 1961").

N. N. Mbile makes a historical museum for any student who is interested in the shadows and reality of Southern Cameroon Politics. Although he has a solemn look, Pa Mbile has a cheerful heart that betrays a distant accommodation one may suspect he has for strangers.

As a veteran journalist, he is prepared to talk with eloquence and grace as he takes you down memory lane. I suppose Victor Julius Ngoh might have found him just too exciting during his interviews with him. Thus the story of Pa Mbile has been told and retold but there are certain features about him that should serve as lessons to the South West Politicians.

He was sometimes an erratic orator whose vision for the future could not be hurdled by obstacles of myopia. Endowed with a political acumen, N.N. Mbile possessed a rare knack for prophecy. He was never bothered to be caught midstream in a pool of controversy and he never minced his words even if that would cost his popularity, for he would rather be remembered for the hard principles he stood for than sacrifice his conscience to the gallery.

Hear him "I, on behalf of the Balondos, would never accept union with the Cameroon republic; if on this we shall have to be killed to the last man, it should rather be better that history records how a race of men died to the man fighting for their freedom".

Whether freedom meant integrating with Nigeria is controversial but this shows the firm and steadfast nature of Pa Mbile and the vindictiveness of politicians for this stand of Mbile resulted in the underdevelopment of his constituency. He was categorical where others sat on the fence and was bold where others became timid.

But what made N.N. Mbile lack the following of a charismatic leader? Many say he has been moving downstream when others are going up-stream and so the truth in him is not judged from the authenticity and credibility of the truth but from the side and ground on which he speaks. N.N. Mbile humorously reminiscences about an experience in Kombone Mission during one of his campaigns in 1960 when one of the citizens said to him "the thing whe dis Mbile di talk ibitru, only na opposition". The political immaturity of the masses could not permit them make a difference between the truth and the votary of truth. And so what came from the opposition was already caged into a negative carton. I suppose it is the experience that made N.N Mbile sceptical about the new political order emerging in Cameroon. And so he took a chance to voice out against multiparty politics at a time when the country was caught in the Euphoria of Pluralism. He advanced credible arguments that made multiparty politics a failure in the 60's and that brought Cameroon into a totalitarian and authoritarian regime in 1966. Mbile warned Cameroonians about the rosy colour that pluralism has facially, but also the thorny value it possesses intrinsically. But the wind of change had blown so fast from the East, the total anatomy of our country had been so bare and no amount of plastic surgery could put the pieces together. The masses therefore lost the culture of reason and swam in the whirlpool of passion believing that their leaders would give them true value of Democracy as practiced in every civilised society. It was yet to be. As lizards joined the chameleons to bask in the sunlight of pluralism, N.N Mbile suggested ideas that could enhance a genuine multiparty democratic process – viz:

(i) The civil service should be non-partisan

(ii) The judiciary and Armed forces should have no partisan political bent

(iii) The public media should be neutral

Today's chaotic state of our democratic march was only proven once more that a people who have learnt nothing in history are worse than people with any history. Note should be made however that Pa Mbile's arguments do not stem from his hatred for democracy but from deep-seated suspicion of the twisted Cameroonian 'democratic' mind. It stems from his experience with the Re-unification "brothers" who say aloud what they do not mean. For indeed, if democracy has to be successful, it must be given and taken in full measures and not applied in half doses. For if there cannot be democracy without democrats, there cannot be a democratic process without setting up democratic structures. Once again, we have failed to give democracy a chance. So caught in this web of confusion, Cameroonians are now in a stalemate. But Pa Mbile has wisely decided not to pay a major role in the new dispensation. While other veterans are still seeking to make or mar their reputations, while some are giving the last kick of their dying political energy, Pa Mbile retreated to the safe adventure of his business. He left the hazardous trade of national politics to upstarts who have refused to find wisdom in his words and inspiration in his actions.

Pa Mbile left the podium of national politics to the dais of local politics as he became concerned with the plight of the Ndian people. Like the Moses in the Bible, he has vowed to take the Ndian people to a promised land where their harnessed resources will be beneficial to them and their divided tongues of Bima and Ngolo will be made to speak the same language of Harmony and Unity. As Pa Mbile gallops along the bumpy road to Mundemba, he reflects on the day that Ndian will be given her rightful place in the map of the South West. But before that day, we may have to read

Pa Mbile's memoirs telling what he calls "the Authentic Story" of yesterday's politics. Hopefully it would not just be a smear campaign that seeks to widen the gulf between the "Endelites" and "Foncharians" but a vivid lesson toward mutual understanding.

That so far has been the history of our heroes. But history has a way of not spotting everybody who partook of the struggle. And so the names of those who made their modest contributions may not have been engraved in the annals of history, but their deeds remain in the chambers of our conscience. For how can one easily forget Motomby Woleta, the eloquent and charismatic speaker who died in 1962? Memories of P.M. Kemcha, S.E. Ncha, and M.N. Foju, still lurk our minds as if they were still with us today.

The status of the seasoned administrator like Jesco Manga Williams, F. N. Ajebe – Sone, E.E Ngone, B.T.B. Foretia still shine though dimly in a distant horizon. Nhon V. E. Mukete, Chief R. M. Ntoko and Chief Nyenti are some of the vestiges of chieftaincy-politics that was the hallmark of southern Cameroon democracy. R. N. Charley, Mabu Bokwe, Pa Kode have left their footprints on the sands of time.

The controversial Walter Wilson will be remembered both for the ink that righted the wrongs in journalism and his VIKUMA creation in politics. He is now considered as a true statesman who fought for the common man against the machiavellian machinations of the elite. What Lobe Nwalipenja, Z. N. Efamba, Bau Okha, D. B. Monyongho and late Nasako, have done to sustain and improve the lives of their people will only be judged by the impartial referee of man's political game – History.

The path that Nzo Ekanghaky, WNO Effiom, E.T. Egbe and Pa Atabong made for this generation may have patches of brambles but it is the duty of this generation to cushion the stress and strain of their penury with the pillows of self-sacrifice.

Since the history of the world is but the biography of great men, the future of the South West lies on the lessons the younger generation will draw from the activities of these historical monuments. Yet the golden question that reputed and respected essayist Tande Dibussi asks still lingers on "How could a province that produced most of the pioneers of West Cameroon political consciousness and nationalism, and that was once at the vanguard of the fight for socio-political freedom become the drum major for political unanimism and authoritarianism?"

CHAPTER THREE

OUR TASK TODAY

The Leadership Question

Leadership is extremely important in the making of any society but it will not give us all solutions to all problems. But as African statesman Olesegun Obasanjo once wrote "if leadership is right, together with the rest of the ingredients that are also necessary, solutions may be brought about. If leadership is wrong and lacks vision, commitment, integrity, honesty, direction and purpose then the chances of success are really slim". We need leadership which links ideas and policy with action. The South Westerner has remained a mere pawn than a major player in the country's chessboard because of economic arrogance, political caution and the intellectual complex. We have always used our natural resources as a trump card in the political game, hoping that when the deal will be done we shall use it to bargain for a more respectful place in our national theatre. Yet since the post-1972 Referendum our transport infrastructure and telecommunication networks have remained the laughing stock of balanced development and a blatant contradiction of the law of derivation. We have rested so much on our economic laurels that we have refused to believe it is he who has the political pipe that calls for an economic tune and not vice versa. That is why Fako, that was once a bustling division now remains a pale shadow of herself; that is why Meme which is the breadbasket of the country still lacks the lustre of an economic division; that is why Manyu with all her unharnessed potentials remains a division of unfulfilled promises; that is why Ndian Division which is the economic lung of the province retrogresses from mediocrity to vulnerability. Yet the South Westerner will publicly point at SONARA, KORUP, PAMOL, CDC etc., etc. as testimony of his economic wealth while he privately laments over his inability to benefit from these giant corporations. True, economy is the foundation of politics but the end purpose of politics is to provide economy. But we have adopted a political caution that seeks to moderate where others are aggressive; we have sought to be apologetic where others are categorical; we have sung the lullaby when others are singing the dirge. And the stark reality today is the more you pressurise, the more you are pampered, for in the battle field of political survival, pressure is the sword of the hero and caution is the shield of the coward. Not even the political parties with a provincial base in the South West have yet made the impact they deserve; for infighting, witch-hunting and personality clashes have been the bane of their existence. Unto us SWELA (South West Elite

173

Association) is born. Its prime mission is to bring about development to the province. For it to succeed, it must first of all get rid of some of those docile barons who have headed this province in the political arena. The leadership does not require the qualities of *"have beens"* or *"wanna-bes"*. Its leadership must not wallow in economic pride or crawl on its stomach to plead for what it deserves; it must not accommodate those who will compromise the objectives of the association with frivolous gains and self-interest. It must bridge the gap between caution and radicalism and transcend the mere rhetoric of hope to the concrete realisation of projects.

The association must bring into its fold a crop of new leaders who will lobby and pressure for what they want rather than hide behind petitions, conferences and memorandums. The leadership must be aware that to achieve economic goals, it must use political means. Rather than blame other provinces (unnecessary xenophobia) for its predicament, its leadership must learn the rules of the game of success. For the haunting nightmare of the South Westerner is this sense of nostalgia or the spirit of looking back in anger; so angry with the road we undertook that we keep stumbling over the same boulders that have retarded our progress so far. Cursing a brother province for taking us mid-stream is not the best given our kind of docility and complicity. Our problems can be solved more efficiently if we pause to conduct agonising self-criticisms and self-examinations to discover the right solution.

To quote Bate Besong "The South West elite has often knuckled under, that is to say he has often failed to dare-even after he has gone there... he has failed to perceive that political power for its own sake is ephemeral. Undoubtedly therefore, the South West elite is the whitlow that afflicts this province whether he knows it or not". And so the elite form a strong intellectual clique with a weak mass mobilisation unit. So SWELA may turn out to be an intellectual association where brainstorming and think-tanking are the rule of the day while mass implementation and task execution become the exception of the night. It may turn out to be a bureaucratic coterie where the shakers and movers of the province feature prominently while the flotsam and jetsam are left in the shadows. Together they must land together or crash apart. The politicians, so far, have not been leaders of the collective will but leaders of their individual opinions; thus their brilliant ideas make reforms at the top without making considerable change at the bottom. The pyramidal structure of power flow has been reversed and the result has been a firm roof on a poor foundation. One of the causes of poor mass mobilisation arises from the inherent trait of our cultural structure. While some provinces are governed by centralised chieftaincies, ours is a dispersed society. In centralised chieftaincies, the chief has considerable influence over his subjects and can pied-pipe them into any direction of his choice. The authority of the chief is manifested through the submission of the subservient masses and the humility of the educated elite. Such unalloyed loyalty means that a chief can wield the destiny of a political party by calling on his subjects to queue behind any politician, depending on the material gain, ideological concept, personal association or tribal affinity the chief has with the politician. The chief, and not the politician, is an instrument of grassroots politics and a facilitator of mass mobilisation. Anything the chief stands for is a symbol of omnipotence and an incarnation of omniscience.

However, as dynamic as the society is, this status quo seems to be fast changing. In our dispersed society there is an absence of centralised government that wields power and authority over the community. With all reverence to the chief, the chief's opinion does not necessarily reflect those held by the subjects. The subjects' unflinching loyalty depends on how sound and convincing the chief's arguments are over any matter of controversy. And so the chief cannot with the wave of his hand order his subjects to line up behind a political leader of his choice. This may sound like contempt of authority or breach of hierarchy; No! It is a celebration of individual belief and the noblest ideal of democracy. Here there is a delicate balance between Respect and Tolerance. Respect of one's opinion and Tolerance towards another's opinion. The second cause for poor mass mobilisation is the colonial mentality of status symbol inherent in our top brass. Here, the colonial legacy left behind was that to maintain respect and exhibit power, the masses must be kept at a distance; a distance that could be wide enough during social occasions but close enough during political campaigns. There is a lack of social interaction between the masses and the politicians because the latter have carved out for themselves a haven of social grandeur while the masse may be stuck in the swamps of penury. And so while the masses visit off-licenses for a drink, the politicians form a social club that by its own creation alienates them from the centre of action that is the masses. The only access card to an elite club is that you must have a name from an institutionalised dynasty or a face from a recognised bureaucratic establishment. As you enter the elite club the question that stares you on your face is "Who are you?" The clubs are for the "some bodies" and off-licenses are for the "no bodies". This colonial status quo was established to widen the gulf between the white masters and their 'inferior' black servants. Today the top brass politicians have attained the status of "white masters" and would not mix with the scum of society. Not that the common man always needs the intimidating presence of a boss around him. No, that saves him the inconvenience of always standing up in respect, the nervousness of chatting in a relaxed mood and the unnecessary servitude of answering "Chief" "Chief" each time the boss intervenes. Yet the truth is that the common pubs are the market places of ideas and the heart-beat of the nation body-politic. Here the politician can record the temperature of his followers and then orientate his priorities.

The story goes that the former President of Guinea, Sekou Toure, wanted to get first-hand information about the welfare of citizens. He disguised as a commoner and went down to the market with the question "What do you think of Guinea?" One of the traders sighed and sorrowfully told him "I wish the Whiteman had not gone" and went to present the catalogue of problems that was besetting the Guinean nation. Sekou Toure must have retuned downcast with a cloud of despair on his face but on second thought he must have let the illumination stars of hope penetrate the cloud of despair, for with the truth gotten from the horses' mouth, the President could now restructure his scale of preferences. The politician needs to come out of his self-made cocoon to meet the common man. For him to accommodate the common man, the boss must be modest but restrained, humble but respectful. In such a common forum, the charismatic politician listens with the ear of a fool but speaks with the voice of a wise man. He engages in a free exchange of common ideas without transforming himself to a megaphone of self-aggrandisement.

Another cause for the gap between the leaders and the masses is the lack of concern for political affairs within the masses (our masses are extremely gullible). Rather than stand up and challenge the validity of an unjust law, the masses often resign to fate and accept the predicament as a token of patriotism. This political apathy may have been as a result of their earlier frustration in the plebiscite cause but in the new dispensation the leaders must be sure that they have a following. It is no use leading a group of people who may abandon you midway in the face of adversity. The masses must respond to the trumpet sound of communalism. A people united can never be defeated. Some analysts say that South West is now "the Thomas of Cameroon Politics - its motto is "Wait and see". Frankly, if the masses have to adopt this obnoxious maxim, then they will never see the political light. Even at grassroots local organisations, the masses do not take initiatives of being at the helm of the office. We cannot content ourselves of always following a path instead of blazing a trail. And so though the South West is central in economic affairs, it is peripheral in political issues; though the breadbasket of economic affairs, it is the waste basket of political refuse. We have nobody to blame but ourselves. Without any political will, one cannot determine the tempo and tenor of development. Olesegun Obasanjo said that for development to be all – encompassing we must release all energy within the community politically, economically and socially.

The trouble with the South West Elite has been the intellectual complex. The Province is blessed with an avalanche of intellectual talents. Right from the time Dr. E.M.L. Endeley said it will take a long time for a brother province to produce a son of his intellectual calibre and fibre; more intellectuals have been born who are almost extinguishing the flame that Endeley sparked.

But the achievements of the intellectual have remained on brilliant ideas than concrete action. This is because there has been more competition among them than consensus. It has always been a case of who should take credit for bringing a good idea instead of which idea could best be implemented according to the realities of the time. Political ideas are like musical notes. When the different notes are carefully organised they produce a sweet melody of blended harmony; but when the notes are distorted, they do not only go off beat or out of tempo, they leave behind a discordant rhythm of cacophony. The intellectuals have been reaching the skies for brilliant ides without touching the ground for concrete realisations. And at a time that we need labour we must turn to the mechanics, the hawkers, the plantation workers, in short the nameless and faceless multitude whose brawn we need to compliment the brains that we have. We need to advance feasible projects that can accommodate our swelling and unemployed wretched of the province or else the status quo whereby our market stalls are occupied by non-natives, our goods are brought from foreign countries, our churches are controlled by others even the houses we live in are built by them; this status quo may continue. But it is not something that has to be reverted by coercion or through xenophobia. No it has to be done by integration and the education of the South Westerner that no job is too menial to be done, and that we must have a commercial mind. We are tired of being a proud but poor people. We shall focus our attention to the farmer, as economically, the objective will be to improve farm to market roads and link all our divisions in the province. This will enhance food production and rural development based on the effective mobilisation of rural communities. The black gold may be simmering in the wells of Ndian or bursting in the pipelines of Fako yet our common destiny lies in our rural population which lives on the abundant commodity of agriculture.

With no credible leadership, Tande Dibussi writes, the province will continue to be "led" by its present leaders who have accepted the province's unenviable role of the cow that is ignored after the extraction of its milk. The province will thus continue to play its unprogressive and passive role of a dejected and helpless spectator on the national political scene.

But my friend Tande, things will change. The present "Leadership" will be passed on to another generation if the province must survive. For the youths have been asked to toe the line when it comes to implementing crucial decisions in the province. This has given rise to a generation gap. The generation gap widens between the young and the old, because the latter still wade in the glory of the past. The importance and contribution of old politicians to our national life cannot be over-emphasised. The records of their achievements or failures are the lamps that guide succeeding generations who may decide to delve into the realm of politics and nation building. Their sense of history makes the old, no doubt, the custodians of our common weal but, not necessarily, the guarantors of our common wealth. The noble role they played in the past has got some of them stuck up in the mire of caution and conservatism while they look at the currents of youthful radicalism as a threat to their own existence. I have attended meetings where the chairman insists on calling me "my son" and then plunging into an epic and ego trip of his "heroic exploits" at a time I was not even born. Another elder refused to buy my first work "**The Mungo Bridge**" on the grounds that a chap as young as me had nothing new to offer him. And we risk letting go this second chance because gerontocracy rides roughshod on the back of meritocracy. We may never see the potentials of youthful creativity as long as we rely on the expertise of ancestral wisdom. We must link our generation gap with a mentality bridge.

The egotist attitude of some politicians whereby only their Kith and Kin can share in the booty of national politics must be discouraged. Some families have enjoyed the monopoly of political lineage proportionate to the Kennedy dynasty in America or the Gandhi caste in India. To these families, I say the growth of this province would not depend on this family pedigree or family-oriented development. The notion of provincial politics goes beyond the narrow confines of the family and embraces the all crystallising forces of individual and mass participation; each son or daughter of the soil must be allowed to contribute his or her own quota not by the fame of his name but by the credit of his merit. The social caste that existed in the pre-72 year in Buea is dead and buried. For as I see it, the leadership of the South West will not come from the folds of a totalitarian dynasty nor from the ranks of an authoritarian gerontocracy. No, the leader would be of humble birth. He will initially be eclipsed by the clouds of conservatism but would gradually rise above this mediocrity to enshrine his name on the marbles of the national pantheon. The South West province has a leader in the making. She has a messiah in the cradle, but for every Jesus Christ, there are going to be two Judas Iscariots and three Pontius Pilates. Such a leader would therefore be armed with courage and conscience, knowledge and wisdom. The chance is given to the youths who unfortunately today are swimming in a whirlpool of unbridled greed. And the legacy of greed has given rise to the heritage of squandermania. The only music that appeals to the heart of the youths is the rhythmic beat of inordinate wealth. They have imbedded the primitive accumulation notion that at the end of the day it is what you bring home that matters, the nation can go to hell. The coffers of the nation can be pillaged and plundered as long as you have a chain of houses and fleet of cars to show for it. I firmly believe that until we know the difference between what we want and what we need, our insatiable thirst for more will never be quenched with a bucket full of a lot more. Man's ego is boundless and not even the centrifugal force of morality can stop it from exploring the wider world of embezzlement and the deeper ocean of corruption.

Our ambitions have been so inextricably bound to the dictates of society that we are no more images of the creator but prisoners of creation. The craziness of the youths today to get more wealth is only taking the universe on the precipice of a moral crisis for as John F. Kennedy said in his inaugural speech on January 20, 1961, "If a free society cannot help the many who are poor, it cannot save the few who are rich". The Youths must forge for themselves a new outlook. Under the new outlook multiplicity of material wants will not be the aim of life, the aim like Mahatma Gandhi says will be rather their restriction consistently with comfort. We shall not cease to think of getting what we can, but we shall decline to receive what all cannot get. To end up May I say this little prayer that Holland said a long time ago in America.

God give us leaders!
A time like this demands strong minds, great
Hearts, true faith and ready hands;
Leaders whom the spoils of life cannot buy;
Leaders who possess opinions and a will;
Leaders who have honour; leaders who will not lie;
Leaders who can stand before a demagogue
And damn his treacherous flatteries without winking!
Tall leaders, sun crowned, who live above the
fog in public duty and private thinking.

May this prayer rise from the heights of the Rumpi hills in Ndian and the zenith of Mount Fako in Fako; may it sink from the depth of Lake Ejagham in Manyu to the bottom of Lake Barombi in Meme.

Cultural Heritage

Talking about cultural heritage at a time when cultural inter-dependence seems to be fast advancing may sound absurd. Like any other African country, Cameroon is at cross-roads of African culture and the many scars of History still remind us of the cultural wounds that were inflicted on us during the scramble for Africa. And so we are torn between two worlds - one of condemnation and the other of Celebration. The first (Condemnation) is seen through the eyes of the colonialist and holds the arrogant view that anything African is inferior and primitive while the second (Celebration) is seen through the eyes of the African and holds the native but naive view that everything African is the "quintessence of human achievement".

These two views have been in conflict in our dresses, handicraft, music, literary work, languages and in all forms of Art. Quite often the colonialist view has gained prominence over our view thereby making our Art second best. Yet Bernard Fonlon says the purpose of culture is to help man to achieve the fullness of his being and thereby real happiness. The genuine seeker after the true, the good and the beautiful which together make up a people's culture will probably arrive ultimately at an acknowledgement of him who is Truth, Goodness and Beauty. The South West Province possesses a diversified culture which like at the national level, cannot be called Provincial culture. Our cultural heritage is like the rainbow whose beauty is seen when the colours are put together and not when they are identified as isolates. Ours is a culture in diversity and it is the display of its mosaic nature that makes us a small global cultural village.

While in Glasgow-Scotland in 1991, it took me time to explain to the Glaswegians, who saw me in what they called a national dress, that there was no particular dress one would call a national dress in Cameroon. Each ethnic group had a way of expressing itself through its dressing mode and with about 236 ethnic groups it was difficult to come up with one particular dressing style and decree it a national costume. However I felt that as the Chinese used their abundant silk to make their silk dresses fashioned after individual taste, so too could Cameroonians use their abundant cotton to make cotton dresses designed after individual appetite.

The Chinese today wear what is produced by them and with their numbers they are able to generate enough local income. When I decided to dress up in what is essentially Cameroon and exceptionally African, two possible reasons were advanced by my friends:

(i) Rediscovery and
(ii) Poverty

The first school of thought lauded the idea of rediscovering the beauty that many undermine, the charm that surrounds us and the futility of searching for the woods instead of the trees. I accepted the idea. The second reason was rooted in the fact that our local wrapper material is cheap and in this time of financial meltdown, I had chosen the easier and cheaper way to weather the economic storm. I also agreed with them for if necessity is the mother of invention, poverty is the father.

As far as I am concerned, I have found a new kind of force that radiates into my soul-the repository of culture, and there is no turning back. Of late women have taken to wrapper materials even though their propensity for foreign wrappers (English Wax, Holland, Nigeria Supper Print) has reduced the Economic value of our local cloth making industries (CICAM, SOLICAM). The mentality goes that the more expensive the material, the more prestigious and the more durable the product. That our local cloth has been erroneously regarded as an inferior material is not only another form of mental slavery, but an arm of cultural suicide. For the wrapper material not only projects the feminine beauty of our female but portrays the multi-colour design that characterises African dresses. The cotton wrapper not only gives a relaxing atmosphere to men but carves out features that would otherwise be hidden in the untropicalised western suits. Our local cotton wrappers are not reserved for the effigies of Presidents and political party identity. They are not exclusively for church associations or social 'ashwabis'. They are all part of our lifestyle. The sporadic outburst of wrapper dresses during social occasions is not enough if we cannot make that dress style our permanent mode of cultural expression. Culture entails a lot of confidence; confidence in what we are and confidence in what we have. The dictum today should be "PRODUCE WHAT WE CONSUME; CONSUME WHAT WE PRODUCE".

Fashion parades could exhibit our home-made material and thus make it a marketable commodity both at home and abroad. The conception that these local products are meant to be exported is absurd. A nation or a person that first of all consumes its own products or finds pride in what it produces give a reason for other people to buy the product. Our challenge is to value our own products even higher than foreign products, for that does not only provide us with a ready-made market but also finds expression in external trade. No matter how much we try to be foreign in our dresses or cultural expression we still remain who we are for as P.M. Kale wrote – 'The British have never in their approach to colonial problems deluded the African, or left him under any illusions that he was an English man; on the contrary what the British have tried to do has been to train the African to admire and emulate the British way of life. The underlying conception of French colonial policy had been "assimilation" or "association" meaning that the overseas territories administered by France formed an integral part of Metropolitan France. But in the final analysis, no self-respecting Blackman wants to be a Frenchman, Englishman or any other nationality, but a good African'. While we continue to overhaul our English language for the sake of international diplomacy we must not play down on our local languages. For though Cameroon is bilingual (official received language) it is against a background of many home languages. In his proposal for an early bilingualism in Cameroon, Dr. Bernard Fonlon wrote:

> I must confess that the expression, Cameroon
> Bilingualism is a misnomer. It would be correct
> to speak of Trilingualism because, even before,
> the Cameroon child comes to school to learn
> English and French; he should have already learnt

his own native language". I must also make it clear that Cameroon's concept of Bilingualism is based on the linguistic concept of received languages (English and French). It is the official reception and recognition of these two languages in the constitution that makes Cameroon a bilingual country, for indeed Cameroon like most African countries has a multilingual and multicultural background, yet it is our two official languages that make us Bilingual. The typical language set up of our country will be coded as HL, + CL, + RL_1 RL_2 that is Home language, Contact language (pidgin) and two Received languages (English and French).

The status of Home language can be raised at individual levels since the fight to make one of our national languages compulsory in our learning process has become controversial. The essential avenue to achieving Home language acquisition is through individual effort at informal level. Maurice Tadadjeu (Cameroonian Linguist) said that "the family is the main source of cultural and moral values and the mother tongue is the key to these values".

Parents therefore have an important task to teaching their children the home language. This can be successful when both parents come from the same tribe or when a compromise is arrived at in case of a mixed marriage. This very important task is embarked on by the mother for she arguably spends more time with the children than the father. It is therefore imperative that mothers impart informally the knowledge of Home language to their children at a very tender age. But with most of the mothers working and the destiny of the children left in the hands of house helps, we are in for a Tower of Babel. It is embarrassing to note today that children even from homes where both parents speak the same home language do not articulate in their home language. The tendency is for parents to communicate in the Home language between themselves while resorting to pidgin or English language when speaking to the children. This is a typical trend in the South West. I had this traumatic experience in my childhood language acquisition. Up till the age of six, I was told I was fluent in my Home language (akose) but because of the marital dissonance between my father and mother, my mother was not around for long to carry forward my home language perfection. I personally dropped the effort of improving on the language as I had very few peers to communicate with. My father's job made it difficult for him to bring us up at home (village) as we kept moving from one administrative unit to another. With a poor communicative audience, unconducive environment and lack of personal effort, I inevitably lost the fluency of my mother tongue. Today, when I stand up to speak 'akose' it is with difficulty and only a native would decipher meaning from my babbling utterances. Nothing is as painful as taking a tribe out of oneself. A man who cannot communicate fluently in his Home language among his people is like an accepted Jew among the Gentiles.

The learning of this Home language is a combination of many factors but the individual himself must make a lot of personal sacrifices (my brothers and sisters are more articulate in the Home language). Lack of communication between parents, separation and Divorce can retard the child's knowledge of the Home language. Apart from the home, the media and the church can revitalise our home languages. Radio Buea has been doing a commendable job in the dissemination of our mother tongues through Vernacular Programmes.

The church could be another avenue for helping the growth of our mother tongues. Local communities must be able to use their languages during formal church services and mass. The Priest or Pastor could conduct the Mass or Service in the language(s) of the local community while the congregation sings in the vernacular. This is already the case in some Catholic and Presbyterian churches in the Province. I have attended Masses where the sweet lyrics of Oroko choir, the melodious tunes of Bakossi tradition and the harmonious bars of Bakweri music have left the Priest with a spirit of angelic presence and left the congregation with a sense of spiritual fulfilment. I hope this trend is maintained and local choirs taken more seriously. I have heard our National Anthem sung in Ejagham. When Television will go Provincial, ours will not pay the kind of lip service our national Television is playing to our cultural heritage.

Another aspect of our cultural heritage is our music. It is evident that music is a vehicle of culture. Our villages abound with rich traditional music diversified enough to entertain a large audience. It is one of the most potent forces in the Province where women and old men excel. Our traditional music still remains unadulterated for it is always being replenished by the vital agents who by themselves are custodians of our rich cultural heritage. However, festivities that warrant the display of our traditional music have become rare and today only political and administrative imperatives call for the exhibition of traditional Music. The lack of lustre in rural life and the search for jobs in urban areas have brought a decline in traditional ceremonies. In the former days, each village had an important occasion that brought together the folks of the village. The villages brought out their best "juju" during this period of initiations and this brought a lot of touristic attraction and cultural solidarity.

Today the pomp and fanfare of traditional music have been reserved for political holidays and V.I.P visits. Hurriedly organised, the dances teach nothing to the young and inspire nothing to the old. It is a mere official routine. Traditional music is rooted in the soul and where there is a lack of total commitment and enthusiasm, the dancers may energetically wring their waists but the dancing will lack the expression that it communicates.

The cry today is for those genuine cultural celebrations in the village to be revitalised. Inter village competition be organised in the divisions, the best from each division are represented for a Provincial competition and then a national festival of Art and Culture can be organised. While the old yearn for pure and unadulterated traditional music, the young yearn for a blend of traditional and modern music to bring their beats to the limelight of international recognition. Other provinces have exploited this avenue but for many reasons the South West Province has not yet produced an artist that has drawn inspiration from village music to produce the brilliance that tradition plus modern blend has. This is not to undermine the works of Sammy Mafany, Jimmy Nyame or Buma Sylvester, but the South West has a rich cultural reservoir from which artists could drink. The first reason for this lack of national and international recognition is the old conservative feeling among the Anglophones that music is for drop-outs. Even though we venerate musicians from other provinces we would want our children to attain university level and get a white collar job rather than allow them wallow in the "hazardous" and "less lucrative" business called Music. And so the children with talents have seen the doors shut in front of them and their creativity nipped in the bud by parents who would love to see their children leaf through the pages of a book than strike the chords of a guitar.

The second reason is the lack of promoters. Artists have been frustrated by the lack of incentives and promotion in the province. It is difficult for an artist to go solo through the conception, realisation and production of his work of Art. The world of Art requires an Artist and a Promoter. We need culturally-minded tycoons to help discover and promote the many talents that this Province has. There is a need for a discipline on Arts to be encouraged in schools and inculcated in the school curriculum.

This discipline would give room for self-expression and an opportunity for children to appreciate the value that traditional music has on our cultural world. Music is one form of Art, the exploitation of our traditional music means the harnessing of other artistic potentials like Plastic Arts, Painting and all forms of handicraft. Local artists must be encouraged. Our household furniture and decorations should reflect the commodities in our local markets. The recognition and appreciation of one's own values is the only way of asserting one's identity. We have looked up to the West for so many things that we despise the beauty that surrounds us. A Friend once asked me how I felt after travelling to Europe. I said the greatest advantage of travelling abroad was that it gave one an opportunity to appreciate one's home better. It made me recognise how much I took my home values for granted. Here was Scotland where a spell of sunshine was a luxury while back home I considered it a nuisance. Here in Glasgow, the sparse vegetation and forest formed a touristic site and a lane for sensuous lovers; back home the forest was an ugly site and habitat for wild animals. We have looked so far for civilisation from the West that we cannot see so near the civilisation from God. And today we do not seem to be inspired even by our own literature. The Anglophone Literature in general has known a lot of paucity while that in the South West in particular still falls below the academic line considering the plethora of intellectuals the province is breeding.

It is common knowledge that great works of Art have been produced by English-speaking countries and so it puzzles one why the same formula does not work with us. Creative writing demands 10% inspiration and 90% perspiration. Therefore even with a little dose of inspiration one can afford to muster some energy to write a book. Yet a few setbacks have made our bookshops and library shelves void of books written by South Westerners. These include:-

(i)   Literary apathy
(ii) Lack of local publishers
(iii) The existence of poor readership.

Most of those who handle the business of publishing do so with mercenary intentions. After the harrowing experience of being duped by a publisher, it takes courage and sacrifice for a writer to publish another work of Art. Few are those publishers who regard the writing trade as an academic exercise meant to lay a solid foundation for posterity.

The frantic quest for wealth by unscrupulous publishers has scared a good number of writers. The printing press is a great asset to the writer. Yet we still rely on neighbouring countries and foreign powers to print our works. With the paper and pulp industry under renovation at Edea, each province should be capable of having a modern and sophisticated printing press. The University of Buea will hopefully regard the printing press as an indispensable tool of learning in the campus. For if our writings must survive the test of time and clime, and then the printing press is a categorical necessity. The avalanche of newspapers and catalogue of books would be irrelevant if there are no people to read them. The reading habit of the Anglophone is an affront to our intellectual status. From the ordinary paper that comes out weekly to the books that are publish periodically, our poor reading stimulus is the same. Our reading audience must be well over a million yet it takes an exceptionally good English newspaper to sell over three thousand copies of its "Thirty Thousand" print run. A writer that succeeds to sell one thousand copies of his books to the Anglophone public in this country must be enlisted in the Pulitzer Award or its local equivalent. Any public that has no interest in books may gradually lose its store-house of knowledge and the treasury of its mind. Books are the compasses that vividly chart the journey of our lives here on earth.

For the writer to sustain his writing, he must be satisfied the books have reached the audience. I remember when I published my first work **"The Mungo Bridge"** a friend walked up to me and congratulated me but regretted that he could not afford 1.000 frs to pay for the book. He however invited me to a nearby pub "to pour his blessings" on the book. He ended up spending twice the cost of my book on drinks he bought for us. Of-course I appreciated his gesture but I thought he had shifted the value from the substance to the shadow. The value of a book is not a momentary appraisal but a lasting appreciation thus the need to stock one's library shelf with as many books as one can find time to read them. Voltaire said "you despise books, you whose whole life is devoted to the vanities of ambition; and the search for pleasure or plunged in idleness; but you should realise that the whole of the known world, with the exception of savage races is governed by books alone".

To justify the importance books have over our lives, public libraries should be built at divisional levels and run by Rural or Urban Councils. We find it difficult today to write our History because we lack memoirs or books to pass over to posterity. The absence of libraries has made it difficult to get access to the few books that talk about our history, and so what we have today are distorted facts and diversified interpretations based on subjective judgements. There are many agencies that are prepared to provide books free to these libraries as soon as these infrastructure are set up. Schools should also make libraries a compulsory facility in the learning process and make them available to students so as to inculcate a spirit of reading. In order to conserve and preserve our cultural industry, public creative agents like Museums, Cultural centres and Art Galleries should be constructed. A people that do not preserve its past may lose its future. Our story is a long one - from slavery to colonialism, from colonialism to neo-colonialism. Every facet of that history must be preserved. Our moveable patrimony must be kept on display and exhibition, for education and touristic attraction. Even before the advent of Television in

Cameroon, the cinema industry was on the decline. It is now becoming clear that while we screen imported films on our television and buy video tapes that portray foreign culture, we leave our talented film stars to be crushed under the weight of cultural imperialism. This province is not yet proud of any film production that reflects the lifestyle of the people of the South West. Some have ventured in the cinema business with pirated war films that aim at reaping fat and fast profit. The artists have been too lazy to walk the journey of cultural introspection. And so arguably today, the best film that has rocked the Cameroonian industry is Daniel Kamwa's "Pousse-Pousse". Any local artist who goes acting Westerns or Kung-fu because that is where the money is will be as absurd as a foreigner trying to portray the impact of polygamy in the Western culture.

For these projects to be feasible, the Ministry of Information and Culture must draw a balance between information and culture or may develop culture into a full-fledged ministry. Meanwhile, the Delegations at Provincial level will not only promote accomplished artists but more so discover potential talents roaming wild on urban streets and running amok in rural squalors.

Save Our Souls

From the time the Whiteman set foot on our soil, he had in mind the possibility of turning our souls to dance to the tempo and tenor of his own culture. And so the gymnastics about Christianity was only a tip of the iceberg that could rock our boat of culture into the deep blue sea of cultural consciousness.

While the existence of a supreme being is unquestionable, the form of his being and the manner of his worship varies from one culture to another. Yet the common denominator is the fact that every group of people has their way of worship – from our vilified way called "Paganism" to their "Glorified" way called Christianity.

Every group of people has their church that responds to the dictates of their faith for it is recognisable that the church is in fact the hospital of the soul and each soul would only look for the doctor that can best diagnose the cure of its spiritual ailment.

We virtually lost our doctors when the Whiteman came with his bible. We tried to understand his new religion but he castigated ours with contempt. He took our soil then went for our souls. But now it is imperative that for any group of people to assert their cultural identity, they must first of all liberate their soul.

We must take ourselves on the altar of self-examination and assess how far the cultural imperialism has eaten deep into the fabrics of our souls. So deep that we are but a people with a hazy past and a confused present. Yet the flag of cultural independence must be hoisted. A new cultural trumpet must be blown rallying us round the table of fraternity, and urging us to sing the sweet songs of unity in a world where cultural dominance is a prerequisite condition for economic exploitation.

We were taught to pray by closing our eyes; when we closed our eyes our soil was raped and our souls wrecked. Today we must pray with our eyes open, for the eyes are the mirrors of the heart and since prayers come from the heart the images must be reflected in its own mirror.

When our souls are tied to the strings of cultural dominance, we become mere pawns in the economic game and puppets in the political theatre.

When our souls are fastened by the grip of cultural dominance, we lose confidence in ourselves and prevent the divine power from radiating the artistic epiphany embedded in us.

When our souls are crushed under the boots of cultural dominance, we yearn to be like everybody else but ourselves; and while we bask in the sunlight of our own mediocrity, the chill of Western culture find expression in our souls and produces at best spasms of a poor cultural "metisasge" and at worst gooseflesh of a rich cultural "blanchissage". Save our souls.

Save our souls from believing that our best is not good enough for the nation and the world.

Save us from believing that we must always follow a path instead of blazing a trail. Save our souls from being the reception of toxic "west" and the reservoir of imbibed cultural junk.

Save us from such damnation.

We are driving on a highway of cultural interdependence. A two-way traffic that must respect the signals that come from both ends, but a man who will not say "I am" will not be told "you are". There must be an assertion of cultural independence before bargaining for cultural interdependence. And this is not mere rhetoric read from the frail pages of a malleable constitution; it is pragmatic action manifested in the daily interaction of our sustainable lives. This is not another poem to be memorized in the soul of our existence. This is not lip service paid on ceremonies untold; it is a life service rendered as the days unfold. It must be manifested anywhere at any time, for you can take a man out of his culture but you cannot take the culture out of him; except he is a soulless animal. But this does not require extreme infatuation with one's own culture or a total annihilation of another person's culture. And so the battle for cultural assertion must go on and the victory lies not on the deadly weapons carried on the body but on the fighting spirit instilled in our souls. As the Japanese technology was built on the ashes of Hiroshima and the debris of Nagasaki, so the victory of our cultural assertion will be built on the rediscovery of ourselves and on the renewed sense of confidence rooted in our souls. As the wave of political tension rises and the tide of social unrest mounts, our souls demand that we become the last pebbles on the democratic shores of cultural assertion. Yes, Save Our Souls.

Environmental Sanitation

A healthy soul can only thrive within a healthy body. The concept of Environmental Sanitation dwells on the need for mankind to live in a clean, comfortable and convenient environment. It dwells on the premise that without a clean surrounding, man will not be able to appreciate the aesthetic and moral values that have been given him by the divine powers.

The concept therefore seeks to raise man's awareness of his environment and the relationship between biotic and non-biotic things. Environmental Sanitation aims at fostering an attitude of care and responsibility to the environment, illustrating the involvement of individuals, organisations and countries in the environment, and changes within it. Without delving into the intricacies and complexities of Environmental Education, we must draw our attention to our cities and villages which are fast becoming a disposal centre for toxic waste. Our basic primary school knowledge of Hygiene and nature study compels us to know the consequences of a dirty environment to our own existence. Yet when we look around our homes, offices, schools, churches, hospitals, and recreational places, this basic knowledge of Hygiene seems to be one of mere rhetoric without concrete realisation. Our homes are found in the midst of overgrown shrubs, littered wrappers, and piled garbage heaps.

Without digging a hole were waste materials can be dumped we stand a risk of making diseases our daily companion and the hospitals an uncompromising friend.

In quarters where neighbours share the same flats it is advisable to construct clean pit latrines safe away from the home and also confer on digging a common hole that will serve the purpose of garbage disposal. This can be done with the strict supervision of medical authorities and local councils. With our sanitation inspectors now out of job, it is clear that our sanitation lies in our hands and decrees or arêtes will not make our living conditions better if we ourselves do not take challenge of keeping our surroundings clean. Straying animals (pigs, goats, sheep) are fast becoming a health hazard and nuisance to public decency.

While the implementation of garbage disposal is individual, the supervision of such a policy must be carried out by some organisations. Firstly the councils have the task of providing garbage cans and litter bins at every strategic site of the street. This will enable citizens to dump their waste at appropriate sites and face penalty if the law is violated. In Scotland, a levy of £25 - £200 is hammered on any citizen caught messing the roads. There are cans and bins at every twist and turn of the town to facilitate waste disposal.

Particular areas should be developed for the throwing of refuse. The refuse could also be burnt in huge incinerators, buried in large dumps and covered with earth or better still sold to farmers as manure. All of this involves finance which most of our councils say they do not have. The purchase of cans and bins can be done by encouraging Companies to use the utensils as advertisement sites whereby each can or bin should carry a sticker, label or logo of a Company. The money accruing from such advert can help in paying the workers responsible for garbage disposal. Citizens themselves must be informed on the importance of Environmental cleanliness, the media (Press, Audio, visual) must make it a duty to sensitize and sensitize the population on the hazards of living in an unchecked surrounding.

It is embarrassing to walk down our streets during the rainy season. Our poor drainage system has made the gutters and culverts stop gap of amassed refuse. The stench and sight of refuse not only nauseates the passer-by but also irritates the environmental conscious citizen. The planning of our towns and villages seem to have no regard for our drainage systems. The conflict of Authority and responsibility over Sanitation between the council and Central Administration (Divisional Office) has aggravated our sanitation problems. I think every council should be vested with full responsibility over Environmental cleanliness within its area of jurisdiction. While this conflict goes on the citizen who pays his taxes but does not enjoy the benefits there from looks stupefied.

Take a look at our markets where we by our food-stuff. It is a disaster. It is an abomination.

A Kumba-based journalist Francis Ndengu graphically and in Ayi Kwei Armah's style vividly portrays Kumba market as follows:-

"Yet all that is nothing to compare with the left-over fufu and Okro-soup that is deposited in the drains under the eyes of the health officers, snails shells and eru that accompany the former, empty cartons of fish and plantain stumps left to decay in the streets, stale bread and beans littering a little too much for the mad ones, etc. etc. This is just a bit of Kumba town at the peak of 20th century".

The market women crawl over pilled refuse just to look for a clearing that will enable them make fast money. The buyer is oblivious of his buying area as he hurriedly goes for what he wants and abandons the site to the poor ladies who must live in such abject squalor just to feed their hungry mouths at home. But who are the buyers? Francis Ndengu continues "This is where the SDO's food is bought. This is where the Mayor of the town derives his food as well; this is where poor farmers who cannot afford a tablet of nivaquine sit down for hours and sell food to the wife of a medical practitioner and not less than 10 metres away, dirty eating houses operating in disgraceful shacks serve food to the public! Here vegetables and cocoyam decay and serve pigs at night. This is Kumba!" Indeed this is Kumba, yet Kumba is just a microcosm of a sanitation unfriendly zone that characterises the rest of the towns in the South West Province. Take a ride down the beach market at Ekondo-Titi and see the wreckage the citizens are exposed to.

Regarded as one of the busiest markets in the South West, the beach market at Ekondo would proudly contest for an award of "Stinking site of the Year" Yet the market man wades in the pool of mud or wallows in the swirl of dust just to hand a market ticket to the poor trader who cannot understand why his levies are unable to fetch him a conducive site for his money's worth. He cannot understand why the money cannot be used to pay workers to clean the market, at least twice a week.

The danger is that when one talks about these sordid and bleak situations, people are prepared to console themselves with the answer that a more grim and gruesome situation exists in the economic and political capitals of this country. And so we have learnt to live in such penury contented that we are not the worst after all. We have learnt by heart the adage that "Black man no di die dirty". So as we leave our homes and walk down the streets to the market daily we only complete a vicious circle of sanitation myopia. The days of well-constructed markets like the one in Tiko, are yet to come and our Administration has remained indifferent knowing that their docile and apathetic citizens will always adjust. And we have adjusted. Our village and towns stink but our noses are held up in the air with the typical haughtiness of a South Westerner who feels it but resigns himself to it.

Our motor parks are pungent sites where jungle justice takes hold over the law of sanitation. Aware of these dangers, local communities have engaged themselves in self-help projects like "keep the community clean" a day set aside for pubic cleaning and sanitary campaigns. On this day offices and business areas are closed and citizens are expected to (once a month) observe the rules of sanitation. The outcome is that either a section of the bush surrounding the office is cut down or part of the mountain refuse is made low. The citizens can now resume their work, while waiting for another rendezvous same time, next month (that is if within the interval an important personality does not come to town). While lauding the administration for the good intentions of such a policy, it must be noted here that the rest of the days of the week are left for individuals to carry on their sanitation obligations. The administration may try to raise Awareness as much as possible but if the individual himself is not convinced of the dangers that befall him, if he does not check his excesses, Environmental sanitation will remain another theoretical concept.

Like Galileo said, you cannot teach a man everything. You can only help him discover it within himself. The need therefore for the individual to be environmentally conscious cannot be overemphasised. The throwing of dirt on the roadway, the dropping of litter on the streets, the piling of refuse in the market, the passing of urine on the roadside and the disposing of garbage around the home must be totally condemned by the individual himself. We must be conscious of the harm that lies ahead of us if such a practice becomes a habit. If the council is to take the responsibility of Environmental Sanitation, then it must look for means of generating income other than levies. The Mayors must not only wait to control budgets, but must use their ingenuity to bring wealth into the coffers of the council.

Non Governmental Organisations should help disseminate the concept of Environmental Sanitation not only within the field of conservation and sustainable development but also in the field of Sanitation and human development. The greatest threat in the Environment today is Man. In a world of poor sanitation man has become endangered species.

Thanks to the courtesy of "The TIDY BRITAIN GROUP" which campaigns for a beautiful Britain, the following axioms may remind us of our sanitation habit.

(i)   Be Street Wise (put your dirt in the nearest bin)
(ii) Prevent Rubbish Spills (don't over fill the bin)
(iii) Tidiness begins at Home (you are clean if your home is tidy)

(iv) A tidy workplace is a safe workplace (if your office is clean it will make the day's work lighter and livelier).

(v) Have a tidy up Day (without waiting for the authorities to decree a day for clean-up, set aside a day that your staff will clean the business area, or office premises).

(vi) Watch the little things (sweet wrappers, bus tickets, cigarettes ends are the little things that make the town dirty; put them in a bin).

(vii) Profit from your image (take pride in your premises, it will improve your image with visitors, customers and the public in general).

(viii) Improve your school Environment. (tidy classrooms, laboratories and staff rooms are safer and ensure a pleasant working environment).

(ix) Be human. (Passing urine and defecating on the road and public places even in the heart of darkness is a sign that our animal instincts still override our human reason).

Making sure the Environment is a safe place to live in is the responsibility of each person in the community. The Public Health authorities may keep a constant watch and may pass laws from polluting our towns and cities. But the implementation of such laws is our responsibility. If we have modern housing and good town planning to include parks and open spaces then we will be making a better and healthier environment for ourselves. We are responsible for our health.

CHAPTER FOUR

OUR COMMON FUTURE

South West: Assembly of Divisions

The South West Province constitutes a group of people who share the same geographical boundaries against a common historical legacy and who share a certain degree of linguistic ancestry against a multicultural background. Though separated by valleys and hills, the administrative divisions in the Province are linked by roads and bridges that should unite them under one umbrella. Yet to say the people of the Province are united will be a white lie. In fact the infighting along divisional cleavages has been sometimes fiercer than the struggle against colonialism. This is the time to bury the differences and highlight the similarities that draw the divisions together. For what is the South West but a melting pot of Ndian tradition, Fako culture, Manyu tradition and Meme culture. It is this diversity that ties the unique identity of the people and it will take only a moron to draw a large dividing line on to the divisional lines that administrators have created in the Province. If an Oroko man cannot feel safe in Limbe or a Bakossi man feels insecure in Mundemba, then our tribal factions would only add insult to our Provincial injury.

Respecting your tribal origin is a great sign of Patriotism but discriminating against another person's tribe is what we refer to as Tribalism. So Tribal Affinity is not a crime per se, it is tribalism that is our canker-worm. Tribalism is also a problem of regional development. When a region has been marginalised and made to play second fiddle, the people inadvertently stand together as an obstacle to National Unity. Therefore there cannot be National or Provincial Unity without balanced development. Tribalism has been aggravated with the advent of capitalism and so while a whole tribe may be persecuted for encouraging the vices that flood our political system, it is indeed a group of egocentric individuals that perpetuate such vices. I refuse to believe that tribal affinity is the woe of African states. No, it is the existence of class structures within our society; for not all members of a particular tribe in power benefit from the fruits of leadership. The leaders from that tribe only build a cocoon around them and would only accommodate their species with the same gluttonous taste for glory, insatiable appetite for wealth and frantic search for power. This is the "nouveau-riche" that wrecks a nation and exposes the tribesmen to the harsh climate of persecution. For what is Africa but a continent of ethnic groups possessing a diversity of traditions and cultures, bound together by the desire to promote Economic, social and political progress and cemented together by the bricks of unity. So a Province that stays together progresses together. The people of the South West Province are bound to stay together if they must progress. Even though each division should highlight the problems that beset her, it must be remembered that what affects one division directly, affects another division indirectly. Through the spirit of planed and collective engagement we shall be able to realise development in a system that now depends on self-actualisation and self-reliance.

South West: One of the Two Anglophone Provinces

When the League of Nations under Article 22 made Southern Cameroons a mandated territory under Britain, it was breaking the umbilical cord that had linked the Southern Cameroons to her German mother since 1884.

This Section, then called British Cameroons, was administered as one of the Provinces of the Eastern Region of Nigeria and was located on the Coast between the Cross River on the West and Mungo River on the East.

After the Plebiscite results of February 1961 and the Reunification Pact in October 1961, this section came to be called West Cameroon in the Federal Republic of Cameroon.

The 1972 Referendum gave rise to a unitary state that split the West Cameroon state into the North West and South West Provinces. Today the North West and South West Provinces constitute the only Anglophone Provinces in Cameroon. Not only do these provinces share the same mother (Germany), they also share a common language (English language). This language similarity carries along with it a common culture and a diversified but complimentary ideology. People with such a common ancestry can only stick together when the ill wind blows and respect each other as reflected in the spiritual vows that accompany matrimony. For some time now, this common ancestry of the North West and South West Provinces is being threatened by the forces of discord. The debate over who did what and what happened when in the West of Mungo politics may not die down yet. But when all men must have spoken their Peace, History which is the greatest communicator and Time the most eloquent orator will also be given their chances to speak their mind.

When the foibles and flaws of the egoistic politicians must have been arraigned in the court of discourse, their verdict will be passed in the court of human conscience. That these two Provinces share a lot in common is a historical fact but that they differ as much is a daily reality.

The end purpose of History will be defeated if it were merely a recording of past events. The purpose of History is to take a look at the past events, correct errors, prepare oneself for the task ahead. For as my village people say "A toad that sets out early in the morning on a journey must from time to time look behind for a hidden enemy". As an old order dies so a new order is born - a new order that must brace itself to face the challenges that these two provinces face in the new dispensation. History is a cyclical event. After some decades a revolution begins and a new generation sets the heart of the world beating; the pulse rate ticks away with the pace and pressure of that generation, then goes back to slumber until another generation can give life to it again. Unto us a new generation is born - a new generation with its own rules and its own intuition. A generation that is prepared to part with their "patriotic" ancestors to forge for itself a future that can accommodate them on the West banks of the River Mungo. The old lyrics of backstabbing and treachery must be buried for hymns of reconciliation and mutual respect to resurrect.

Common sense demands that the two Provinces look at their past as a comedy of errors and interpret the future as a testament of hope. For, indeed the cornerstone of National Unity lies on the Anglophone foundation. The divide and Rule system may be a political ploy to wreck the cultural spirit of oneness; but it is a social blunder toward political stability, for it is only the inherent moderation of the South Westerner that can check the radicalism of the North Westerner and it is only the innate radicalism of the North Westerner that can balance the moderation of the South Westerner.

From 1961, the two Provinces have built a tower of Babel between them and thereby lost their Garden of Eden.

My message to the South Westerner is that he may conveniently wallow in his Economic virtues but would need the North Westerner as human resource. For the ingenuity and industry of the North Westerner has made them the David's of Cameroonian Politics. Yet the North Westerner must eliminate his backstabbing technique if he has to share an apartment with his South West brother. Stories are still rife where Posts of responsibility meant for the Anglophone have been monopolised by the North Westerner. Stories are still with us where some top ranking officials from the brother province have discriminated against the South West.

Stories are still with us where the North Westerners will pull together as brothers even if it means ruining the Anglophone edifice. I suppose some of the same crimes must have been committed by some South Westerners against their North West brothers. Worse still who is not familiar with the backstabbing and discrimination among South Westerners? Such are the enemies of the New Dimension. But a worse enemy is a new crop of Assimilated Anglophones. This breed has been attracted by the magnet of linguistic majority. The linguistic osmotic pressure has drawn them to the Francophone majority solution that they speak French with the fluency of the Francophone and contempt for anything Anglophone. They are Anglophones by birth but Francophone by survival. They have even replaced the linguistic concept "Anglophone" with a political theory "Cameroonian" taking this for a sign of Patriotism. I firmly believe that to accept the appellation "Cameroonian" is the highest degree of Patriotism but to refuse the appellation "Anglophone" is the lowest degree of cultural detribalisation. For "Anglophone" is our linguistic origin and "Cameroonian" our political destiny. A lesson from the African-Americans in the United States of America tells us that they have realised today that until they drink deep from the fountains of their African origin, their thirst for an American identity will never be quenched. And so the Anglophone must shout his "Anglotude" on the roof top without feeling guilty of subversion. For indeed if the seeds of treachery and the element of distrust continue among the Anglophones, it would only make the North Westerner

221

play the window dresser and the South Westerner play the onlooker as other provincial comedians continue to make a burlesque of our National Politics.

Yesterday's actors were Jua, Egbe, Muna, Endeley, Foncha, Kale Mbile, S.A. George, Fon Achirimbi etc. Their plots were poignant with insinuations and witch hunting and pregnant with emotional wrangles and egocentrism.

As the drama keeps unfolding, the call for today's actors is to be more intellectually mature and politically tolerant. The quality traits ingrained in the English system permit the Anglophones to strike a better deal that can allow them walk on the corridors of leadership. The Anglophones must unite not as a separate entity but as an integral block within the mainstream of Cameroonian Politics. The journey toward genuine Cameroonian National Unity would only begin with the first step of Anglophone solidarity, for Anglophone solidarity is not only vital for the survival of the Anglophone themselves but necessary for the existence of all of us – Cameroonians.

South West: One of the Provinces of Cameroon

The creation of the Unitary State in 1972 gave rise to seven provinces, and in 1984 for the purpose of smooth

Administration three more provinces were created bringing the number to ten. South West therefore is only one of the ten provinces that make up the socio political entity called Cameroon.

She must not in her quest for development carve for herself a political niche independent of the country's anatomy. If each province concentrates on auto-development without any distrust for another province, the ultimate goal will be balanced development and economic prosperity. The quest for a Federated structure is a National issue and if it is the system that may bring prosperity to Cameroon, then the South West must make bold to clamour for it. Trying to address South West issues only without attempting to condemn some of the obnoxious and ignoble laws that rule over Pax Cameroona will be tantamount to bandaging an abscess without taking a pain killer to relieve the whole body. We are all but fragments in a web of unity. We are inextricably bound to each other and though our Provinces may be separated by land and water the people are united by body and soul. The daily interaction of our citizenry is testimony to the fact that no province can arrogate to herself the powers of supremacy – not even the Province from which the President of the country comes.

For long the South West had refused to be in the vanguard of a national battle, she has at best shied away from issues that are controversial and at worst sat on the fence or even backed the wrong political horse. In the attempt of becoming an honest broker she may end up becoming an honest loser.

And for the sun of Economic Prosperity to shine, there must be the blue sky of Political stability. The stability and unity of this country should not be compromised in any way by a province that prides herself to being the Economic lungs of this country. Otherwise the Province will be as absurd as Chinua Achebe's proverbial lizard that ruined his own mother's funeral; and the people of that Province will be as suicidal as the man who killed his hen that laid the golden eggs.

All provinces form the links that make up the bright chain of Cameroon. When each link is firmly tied to each other it gives a kind of strength that cannot be broken. But when the chain has a missing Link, the missing link that stabilises the strength of the other links of the chain, that chain becomes vulnerable. For the chain of Cameroonian Unity to be solidified, the missing link of the South West Province must be energised. It is the task of all South Westerners to whom the Province politically belongs and the duty of all Cameroonians for whom the Province's Economic bells jingle.